From the first tee to the 18th green—here is golf at its wacky worst:

THE GOLF HALL OF SHAME

Q. Why did golfers carry guns at Yellowknife Golf Club in Canada?

A. To stop ravens from stealing their golf balls. *(See page 26)*

Q. How did Mac McLendon make history at the 1979 Masters?

A. His tee shot hit his wife in the gallery. *(See page 120)*

Q. What happened to golfer Les Madison at the 1936 U.S. Open?

A. His pocket was picked by a sticky-fingered spectator. *(See page 83)*

Q. Where did Michael McEvoy put his drive from the third tee during a 1922 tournament in Ireland?

A. Into a donkey's ear. *(See page 124)*

Q. Why didn't Porky Oliver make the playoffs in the 1940 U.S. Open, even though he had tied for the lead?

A. He was disqualified for teeing off too soon. *(See page 147)*

Books by Bruce Nash and Allan Zullo

The Baseball Hall of Shame™
The Baseball Hall of Shame 2™
The Baseball Hall of Shame 3™
The Football Hall of Shame™
The Golf Hall of Shame™
The Sports Hall of Shame™
Baseball Confidential™
The Misfortune 500™

Published by POCKET BOOKS

THE GOLF
HALL OF SHAME™

BRUCE NASH AND ALLAN ZULLO
TIM ROSAFORTE, CURATOR

POCKET BOOKS
New York   London   Toronto   Sydney   Tokyo   Singapore

Over the years, *The Rules of Golf* have evolved and changed. In recounting the stories in this book that involve rules, we refer to whatever rule was enforced at the time of the incident.

An *Original* Publication of POCKET BOOKS

 POCKET BOOKS a division of Simon & Schuster
1230 Avenue of the Americas, New York, NY 10020

ISBN: 0-671-74583-2

First Pocket Books trade paperback printing November 1989

10 9 8 7 6 5

Printed in the U.S.A.

DEDICATION

To my lifelong best friends, Randy Monchick and Jim Graham, whose extraordinary golfing skills unfortunately never rubbed off on me.

—B.N.

To the two most beautiful duffers in my life, Allison and Sasha Zullo.

—A.Z.

ACKNOWLEDGMENTS

We wish to thank all the players, caddies, tournament officials, and sportswriters who contributed nominations.

We are especially grateful to those players on the PGA, LPGA, and Seniors tours and the retired pros who shared a few laughs with us as they recounted the inglorious moments that earned them places in The Golf Hall of SHAME.

This book couldn't have been completed without the outstanding assistance of researcher Barbara Arnold, golf historian Dawson Taylor, and our curator, Tim Rosaforte.

We also appreciate the special efforts of Janet Seagle and Karen Bednarski of the USGA's Golf House museum and library; Pete Wofford and Kathy Gallagher-Jorden of PGA of America; Denise Taylor and Ric Clarson of the PGA Tour; Tim Crosby of the Senior PGA Tour; Sandi Owen, Julie Gumlia, and Elaine Crosby of the LPGA; and Rich Skyzinski of the USGA.

In addition, we want to thank all the golf writers, historians, officials, and others who provided us with needed information and material. Special thanks go to: Blair Dickinson, Larry Dorman, Gordon Glenz, Sheila Grattan, Helen Hagen, Ken Hambleton, Terry Holt, John Hopkins, Ken Janke, Keith Mitchell, Jeane Munday, Sara Noah, John Riley, Rick Schloss, Chris Smith, Jack Sneiderman, Dick Taylor, and George White.

We especially want to thank *Golf* magazine and *Golf Digest* for material which enhanced some of our stories.

And for steering us clear of the roughs and hazards so we could finish this book, we give our love to our playing partners in life, Sophie Nash and Kathy Zullo.

CONTENTS

TEEING OFF

In our 1987 bestseller *The Sports Hall of SHAME,* we devoted a whole chapter to golf, chronicling two dozen great ignoble incidents on the links. For example: At the 1938 U.S. Open, Ray Ainsley shot a record score of 19—for one hole. In one of his first tournaments, Gary Player got knocked out by his own ball. And Hale Irwin blew the 1983 British Open when he whiffed a three-inch putt.

As we toured the country promoting *The Sports Hall of SHAME,* we were surprised by the incredible fascination fans have for golf. Of all the sports, golf is the one that generated the most requests for stories from us on our TV and radio appearances. We soon realized that this game—which makes millions of dollars for the par-birdie-par pro and brings weekends of joy to the slice-your-drive, cut-your-Titleist weekend hacker—deserves its own book of shame.

The history of this centuries-old sport boasts a rich heritage of zany moments from tee to green. To chronicle these priceless incidents, we first visited the United States Golf Association's Golf House in Far Hills, New Jersey, which holds the world's largest collection of books, journals, and publications on golf. We sifted through record books, archival material, and faded newspaper accounts. Next, we gleaned the files at the headquarters of the Professional Golfers Association of America, located in our own backyard of Palm Beach Gardens, Florida.

Then, with the help of our curator, Tim Rosaforte, golf editor for *The Palm Beach Post,* and our golf historian, Dawson Taylor, we interviewed golfers on the PGA, LPGA, and Seniors Tours. We caught up with them at the 1988 Nabisco Championships of Golf, 1988 Chrysler Team Championship, 1989 Doral Ryder Open, 1989 LPGA Oldsmobile Classic, and the 1989 PGA Seniors Championship.

Arnold Palmer, golf's greatest living legend, took time out during the PGA Seniors to recall with a laugh his most mortifying time, when he shot a disastrous 12 on the final hole of the 1961 Los Angeles Open. Jack Nicklaus smiled proudly when he recalled his greatest prank—dumping horse manure in the back of his friend's car in a "payback." And Greg "The Shark" Norman sheepishly talked about his most embarrassing moment on the green, when he hurled his ball in anger—and accidentally nailed playing partner Fred Couples right in the stomach. One of the newest stars of the PGA Tour, Mark Calcavecchia, was delighted to tell his wackiest moment on the course—he picked up at the 1986 Kemper Open after he fell in the mud. He said that story was always good for a laugh.

All the new inductees—from Sam Snead and Chi Chi Rodriguez to Pat Bradley and Payne Stewart—shared a few chuckles with us as they relived their moments of infamy. It didn't matter if they were big names or not. Perhaps that's because time has a way of throwing a humorous light on most any embarrassing moment.

Our ongoing research into golfing shame uncovered many little-known hilarious happenings, from country club tourneys to the prestigious majors. Some of the stories we researched turned out to be apocryphal. For example, time and again we heard that Tommy Armour hit ten straight balls out of bounds at the Shawnee Open a week after he won the 1927 U.S. Open. Upon further checking, we learned the truth—he carded "only" an 11 on the 17th hole in the third round.

One story that we desperately hoped was true also involved a Shawnee tournament. Supposedly, some time before World War I, a woman shot a whopping 166—for one hole! The story had been repeated in several publications and books, including the *Guinness Book of World Sports Records*. But none of them had a date or even a name. After diligent research failed to verify the account, we considered the story just a local legend. But then, a week before our manuscript deadline, with the help of our researcher, Barb Arnold, we uncovered the truth. On one hole, Mrs. J. F. Meehan shot 161 in a 1913 tournament, making her the star of the quintessential *Golf Hall of SHAME* story.

Just what does it mean to be in *The Golf Hall of SHAME?* It's a special recognition of a moment we can all identify with—and laugh about—because each of us has at one time or another screwed up. As long as athletes continue to make funny mistakes, we will continue to chronicle the rib-tickling embarrassing moments in sports as they happen. We won't play favorites. We will faithfully and mirthfully dishonor both the heroes and the zeroes. As our motto says, "Fame *and* shame are part of the game."

SHANKS FOR
THE MEMORIES

Disaster, like lightning, can strike duffers or pros at any time, anywhere on the golf course. Even the greatest linksmen at times play a hole so horrendously that the flag on the green is lowered to half staff. For "The Most Incredible Disasters in Golf History," The Golf Hall of SHAME *inducts the following:*

Mrs. J. F. Meehan
1913 Shawnee Invitational for Ladies

In the most ridiculous, outrageous golfing performance in tournament history, Mrs. J. F. Meehan shot an unbelievable 161—for one hole!

Golf's most stupendous disaster occurred during a qualifying round of the 1913 Shawnee Invitational for Ladies at Shawnee-on-the-Delaware, Pennsylvania. Mrs. Meehan, of Philadelphia, set this stand-till-doomsday record at the 126-yard par-3 16th hole. To reach the green, a drive must carry over the Binniekill River, a branch of the Delaware River.

Unfortunately for Mrs. Meehan, her tee shot fell way short and splashed into the water. Although she could have teed up another ball, she chose to play it out. Turning to her husband, who was standing in the gallery, she shouted, "Get a boat!"

Without stopping to question the wisdom of her decision, Meehan, like a dutiful spouse, scampered down the bank to the water's edge and commandeered a rowboat that belonged to the country club. The boat often was used by a young man who fished errant golf balls out of the water.

By the time the Meehans had climbed into the boat, the ball, which was light enough to float, began drifting downstream away from the hole. With her husband rowing as hard as he could, Mrs. Meehan finally caught up with her ball, which was bobbing in the water about 50 yards from shore and about 100 yards from the green.

Wielding her mashie (as a five-iron was called back then), Mrs. Meehan knelt in the bow of the skiff, leaned over the side, and took a swipe at the ball. All she got for her efforts was drenched. The ball, meanwhile, kept floating merrily on its way.

"That's stroke two," said her husband, who had been looking over her shoulder.

"I know it," she replied coolly. Spotting the ball several yards away, she shouted, "Hurry or we'll lose it!" Her husband quickly maneuvered the boat into position and Mrs. Meehan again swung at the ball, sending up a huge geyser. But the ball just squirted farther downstream.

"That's stroke three and you're getting me wet," said her husband. "You would get along better with a crab net."

"I'm playing golf, not fishing," retorted Mrs. Meehan.

As the gallery followed this watery odyssey from the banks of the river, Mrs. Meehan continued to slap at the river and the elusive ball. After each stroke, her tiring, wet, sweaty husband diligently rowed the boat into another new position, all the while keeping track of her ever-mounting number of strokes. Finally, after more than 40 strokes, Mrs. Meehan managed to beach the ball.

According to a contemporary account in the *New York Herald*, "Panting for breath, the couple stood on the sand, scarcely knowing which way to turn next, as they found thick woods confronting them. Here, again, Meehan proved of valuable assistance to his life partner. . . . Husband led the way, while wife and caddie, who had joined the party after the boat landed, followed, or rather, tried to follow.

"Imagine playing a golf ball through woods. Of course, it was slow work, but after being stymied many times by trees, the trio finally came in sight of the green. 'A few more shots now and your ball will be in the hole,' said Meehan encouragingly.

"A few? Well, not exactly, for the approach that should have made the green landed the ball in a deep place between two rocks. . . . The lie was almost unplayable, yet Mrs. Meehan, either heedless or forgetful of the rule allowing one to tee [take a drop] for the loss of two strokes, kept banging away. A dozen strokes, more or less, at that stage of the game was a mere 'bag of shells.' Somehow, the plucky player did finally get clear, reach the green and hole out, the putt that found the bottom of the cup being stroke number 161."

Although the hole measured only 126 yards long, it was estimated that Mrs. Meehan's ball—with its Binniekill voyage and the zigzag course through the woods—traveled at least 500 yards.

"The woman's feat required something like half an hour," said the *Herald*. "Thereafter, the task of covering the remaining holes was child's play by comparison, and when the smiling, but tired Mrs. Meehan handed in her card, the grand total read—but why rub it in?"

Arnold Palmer

1961 Los Angeles Open • 1964 Bing Crosby National Pro-Am

If Arnold Palmer's actions at the 1961 Los Angeles Open had been on the battlefield, "The General," as Arnie's Army fondly calls him, would have been busted to buck private.

He shot an atrocious 12 on one hole—after blasting four straight balls out of bounds.

As the defending U.S. Open and Masters champion, Palmer was leading another patented charge coming to the 508-yard par-5 ninth hole at Rancho Park Golf Course. It was his finishing hole for the second round and he was gunning for a birdie which would put him only two shots behind the leader.

AP/WIDE WORLD PHOTOS

3

After hitting a good tee shot, Palmer ignored conventional wisdom calling for a lay-up shot to land where the fairway narrows to a bottleneck at the green. Instead, he hauled out his three-wood and gave the ball a ride.

At first Palmer thought he hit a good shot. But the ball drifted to the right, hit the top of a 30-foot-high chain-link fence that bordered the fairway, and landed in the nearby driving range. That cost him one penalty stroke, so he dropped another ball and aimed for the green once again. The ball soared majestically—but it, too, sliced out of bounds onto the driving range.

Another penalty stroke, another dropped ball. This time he made an adjustment and, sticking with his three-wood, blasted away. At least this ball didn't go into the driving range. Instead, it hooked to the left, way off the course and clear out to Patricia Avenue. Palmer was no longer concerned about his runaway score. This had turned into a personal battle: Palmer vs. the ninth hole. After another drop and penalty stroke, he swung that three-wood for the fourth time. It was an exact repeat of his previous hook shot into traffic.

Now lying nine, Palmer still stuck with his three-wood and finally hit a straight ball onto the green. From there, he two-putted for an inglorious 12—the worst score Palmer ever recorded for one hole in a tournament. "It was a nice round figure, that 12," he quipped. "This should give the duffers a bit of heart."

In dishonor of this shameful feat, a bronze plaque on a stone pedestal was installed at the ninth hole to remind all weekend hackers that at times they, too, can be just as "good" as Arnold Palmer. The plaque reads: "On Friday, Jan. 6, 1961, the first day of the 35th Los Angeles Open, Arnold Palmer, voted Golfer of the Year and Pro Athlete of the Year, took a 12 on this hole." (Palmer participated in the dedication with his usual gracious good humor.)

However, the most talked about Palmer debacle happened at the 17th hole at Pebble Beach during the 1964 Bing Crosby National Pro-Am. He was literally on the rocks.

On the 218-yard par-3, which runs toward the sea to a green flanked by rocks and the Pacific Ocean, Palmer hit his tee shot over the cliff behind the green, into shallow water in front of the 18th tee. The bay and its beaches were then played as part of the course. They were not lateral water hazards which would have allowed a golfer to drop the ball on dry land with a penalty stroke. (The local rule was later abolished and the beaches are now considered water hazards.)

As a nationwide TV audience watched, Palmer stood there, with a stray dog watching him curiously, and pondered his shot. Roving TV reporter Jimmy Demaret told viewers the options under the unplayable ball rule: "If he takes the option of dropping behind the point where the ball rests, keeping in line with the pin, his nearest drop is Honolulu."

Palmer gamely swung away on the rocks as his ball bounded from one rock to another. Steam from his head rose with each futile stroke. It took him six shots to get the ball on the green in a seventeen-minute drama captured by the TV cameras.

That same nasty hole vexed Palmer a year earlier, when his two-iron shot flew over the green and disappeared, apparently lost in the water.

Invoking the lost-ball rule, Palmer hit another shot from the tee. But when his first ball was found lying on the rocks on the beach, he played that onto the green. The next day, PGA officials ruled that Palmer had struck an unauthorized provisional ball—that he, in effect, had abandoned his first ball by hitting the second. He was disqualified, even though he had finished the final round. As a result of his DQ, Palmer's string of 47 consecutive tournament finishes in the money was over.

Tommy Nakajima
1978 Masters Tournament   1978 British Open

If any pro golfer has reason to suffer from triskaidekaphobia—the fear of the number 13—it's Tommy Nakajima.

He tied a record for the most shameful one-hole score in the history of the Masters. At Augusta National in 1978, he shot a horrendous 13 on, of all holes, the 13th.

Tommy, a Japanese professional whose given name is Tsuneyuki, which means "always happy," was anything but that after his second-round disaster on the 475-yard par-5 13th.

Gunning for an eagle on the slight dogleg, Nakajima tried to cut the corner with his tee shot. But his drive caught a branch and dropped into Rae's Creek, which snakes along the left side of the woods bordering the fairway. After his penalty drop, he played a five-iron to within 100 yards of the green.

But then adversity struck again. He sent a weak wedge shot into the creek that fronted the green. From there, he tried a recovery shot. The ball popped up in the air and then fell back down—right on Nakajima's foot. Now he was saddled with two more penalty strokes.

Well, he thought philosophically, it can't get any worse. Oh yes it could. Shaken by his troubles, Nakajima tried to give his now-muddy wedge to his caddie to clean, but the pair muffed the handoff and the club tumbled into the water. For grounding a club in a hazard, Nakajima incurred another two-stroke penalty. At this point, even though he had taken four shots on the hole, he was lying nine.

Mustering as much mental strength as he could for damage control, an exasperated Nakajima still couldn't contain all his frustration. He rocketed his next wedge shot over the green. With his spirit all but crushed,

he humbly chipped onto the green and two-putted for his history-making 13.

"I don't like to recall unpleasant occurrences," Nakajima said later. "I had promised myself to make an eagle on that hole. But I tried too hard and messed up."

Three months later, at the British Open at St. Andrews, Nakajima hoped his luck would even out. Among the contenders in the third round, Nakajima was putting for a birdie three from 30 feet away on the 17th hole. He tapped his putt and then watched in dismay as the ball rode the break of the green and trickled off into the feared Road Bunker.

Once, twice, three times, he tried to blast it out of the sand with no luck. "That bunker was so deep and the side was so steep, it was like a wall," he recalled. "I was so mad." Finally, on his fourth recovery attempt, he made the green and then two-putted to close out a golfing horror now known as "The Sands of·Nakajima." He was too stunned to believe it. Moments earlier he had putted for a birdie three; now he staggered off the green with a shocking nine.

For the second time in three months, Tommy Nakajima had been eliminated from a major tournament by a mortifying disaster.

Al Chandler

1986 Senior Tournament Players Championship

In baseball, three strikes and you're out. In golf the same held true for Al Chandler who, on one calamitous hole, whiffed the ball *three* times. By the time he regrouped, he was out of contention and out of the money.

Chandler's startling misfortune came during the 1986 Senior Tournament Players Championship at Canterbury Country Club outside Cleveland. He was among the leaders in the final round, paired with one of his heroes, defending champion Arnold Palmer.

At the par-4 15th hole, Chandler was one under for the tournament and on track to collect one of the biggest paychecks of his career. But then he ran into trouble when his second shot landed about one foot from a huge oak tree that stood ten feet from the green. With the ball between the green and the tree, there was little room for his backswing.

Chandler studied his dilemma. He could turn his back to the green and try to ricochet a shot off the bark and hopefully onto the green. Or he could turn sideways, chip away from the tree, and play for a bogey. Sensing that big payoff, Chandler decided to go for a par, figuring that if he cut down on his backswing he'd have just enough room to pitch the ball onto the green.

But he miscalculated. His club struck the tree on the backswing and he missed the ball completely. But apparently he didn't learn his lesson

7

because he tried the identical shot again . . . with the same results. Another whiff. Incredibly, Chandler tried the same shot a third time. He finally found success—if nudging the ball a measly foot can be considered success. From there, he chipped onto the green 18 feet from the hole.

"Then came the killer of all killers," Chandler recalled ruefully. "I putted up to a half inch, and when I reached around Palmer's mark to tap in, I hit the green behind the ball and missed. I had whiffed three times on the same hole! I couldn't believe it. I came into that hole one under, and I finished four over. It's a wonder I didn't have a heart attack. It's a wonder I finished the round."

Chandler, who scored an embarrassing quintuple-bogey nine on the hole, added, "It wouldn't have been so bad if Arnold Palmer hadn't been standing there. Because of the shock I was in, he tried to be nice to me. He waited until we walked off the 18th green before patting me on the shoulder. I was incoherent. I had just blown five or six grand."

Instead of finishing close to Palmer, who collected $18,750 for third place, Chandler tied for a lowly 32nd, to pick up a check for only $2,137.50.

"Thank God my disaster wasn't on TV," said Chandler. "The cameras were on me immediately before and immediately after. When the TV guys saw on the scoreboard that I had gone from one under to four over, they were calling to their reporters all over the course, asking, 'What happened to Chandler?' "

Philippe Porquier

1978 French Open

In the worst case of the shanks ever suffered by a pro golfer, Philippe Porquier carded the highest score for one hole in the history of the European Tour—an incredible 20!

Playing in his first major tournament, the 1978 French Open at La Baule, the young assistant golf pro was understandably nervous. But he managed to shoot well enough to stay within a few shots of the leaders at the turn of the first round.

At the 511-yard par-5 13th hole, which featured a dogleg to the right up a stiff incline, Porquier impressed his veteran playing companions with a long, straight drive and a nifty three-wood shot that left him a mere 40 yards short of the green.

Swelling with confidence, Porquier had visions of making a decent chip that would set him up for a birdie. But he wasn't really psychic or he would have foreseen an impending disaster never before experienced by a pro on the European Tour.

The harbinger of doom came on his pitch shot. Porquier carelessly struck the ball on the hosel of his nine-iron, causing the ball to fly off the inside curve of the blade at a sharp right angle. His ball rocketed diagonally out of bounds.

Hoping against hope that this was some minor aberration to an otherwise creditable round of golf, Porquier dropped another ball and tried again to pitch onto the green. But to his horror, he shanked this ball, too, into the rough by the boundary fence. With his mechanics all screwed up, his psyche blew a fuse. He kept telling himself over and over not to shank. So naturally he shanked his third straight shot, this time through the fence.

With the penalty strokes, he was now playing eight. But before this nightmare ended, he needed a pocket calculator to keep track of his score. After adjusting his stance, changing his grip, and making a silent vow not to shank, Porquier swung again. He didn't shank this one. He topped it. The ball rolled weakly a yard deeper into the rough. But then he returned to his old form and shanked the next two, one of which went out of bounds again.

As Porquier was about to play his thirteenth shot, his caddie planted himself out of bounds so that he'd have an easier time of retrieving the next errant ball. Meanwhile, Porquier apologized to his playing partners for unduly detaining them. Then he swung and shanked . . . swung and shanked . . .

Suddenly, from the deepest regions of his tormented mind, sprang an idea that he felt surely would bring him salvation. For his eighteenth shot, Porquier took aim not at the 13th green, but at the next tee, which was off to the left side of the green. Then he repeatedly told himself, "Do not shank . . . do not shank . . ." and when he swung, he did his damndest not to shank. Sure enough, his idea worked. The ball shanked, darting sideways from his point of aim, and landed on the green ten feet from the cup.

Porquier smiled shyly as the spectators applauded his cunning strategy. Two putts later, Porquier's name was etched in the record books as the holder of the highest score ever for one hole on the European Tour.

Singing the Blues

Singer Johnny Mathis was playing golf at Moor Allerton in Yorkshire, England, with some British companions when he faltered badly on the eighth hole.

He socked his first drive out of bounds. The second tee shot soared over the trees out of sight. His third drive went even farther, but, alas, it too was never seen again.

Muttering to himself, Mathis determinedly teed up another ball, only to send that to bye-bye land as well. His fifth ball tailed off into a bush, but at least it could be recovered.

As his group walked down the fairway, Mathis lagged behind. Suddenly, his smooth, silky voice filled the air as he sang the musical scale, ending triumphantly on the highest note. When his playing partners wheeled around in wonderment, Mathis told them, "Thank God I can still sing."

What's the Name of This Game?

The first time that Frank Sinatra played golf with Arnold Palmer in Palm Springs, Old Blue Eyes spent more time in the rough than in the fairways.

After the round, Sinatra asked Palmer, "What do you think of my game?"

"Not bad," Palmer replied. "But I still prefer golf."

As a Golfer, He's a Real Lemmon

For twenty-five straight years, terrific actor but lousy golfer Jack Lemmon has failed to make the cut at the Bing Crosby Pro-Am.

The tournament has not been kind to him since his first outing in 1965. "I was so nervous during my first Crosby that I couldn't stay still over the ball," recalled the Academy Award winner. "My caddie, a seasoned veteran, had gone into shock over my poor playing.

"By the 18th, I was averaging eight or nine strokes per hole. On the last hole, I hooked my first drive into the ocean, sliced my second drive out of bounds across the fairway, and popped my third drive up and barely onto the fairway. Three shots later, I hit a nine-year-old kid on the wrist. I went over to the gallery to see if he was hurt, and he asked me if I was insured! I finally got on the green in 11. Looking at a 35-foot putt, I asked my caddie, 'Which way do you think it will break?' He told me, 'Who cares?' "

PUTTING ON THE FRITZ

Golfers hate to three-putt, but at times that can be an achievement. After all, when putting, the linksman might encounter a sudden case of the yips or a green that reads like a Dickens novel. Consequently, the putting arenas have been the stage for some unintentionally classic vaudeville. For "The Most Embarrassing Performances on the Green," The Golf Hall of SHAME inducts the following:

Brian Barnes

1968 French Open

In one of the most atrocious putting performances ever, Brian Barnes took an incredible 12 strokes while putting from only three feet away from the cup!

Up until then, Barnes, a British Ryder Cup player, had played well enough to keep his name on the leader board early in the second round of the 1968 French Open at Saint Cloud. But then trouble flared up on the short par-3 eighth hole. He bunkered his drive and hit a weak chip shot that left him with a long putt and a short temper. Swearing under his breath over his poor recovery shot, Barnes stroked an equally bad putt that rolled dead three feet short of the cup.

Barnes, who at the time possessed one of the surest putting strokes on the continent, felt the steam of anger rising from the back of his neck when his bogey putt lipped out of the cup. It's at a time like this when a golfer needs to step back and find his composure.

Instead, Barnes lost it. What happened next shocked the gallery and his playing partners, who were about to witness temporary insanity on

the green carpet. First, Barnes tried to rake the ball into the hole like some irate Monte Carlo croupier at the craps table. But it was no dice holing out.

So Barnes, who had played hockey in his youth, switched tactics and turned his putter into a hockey stick and batted the ball back and forth—while it was still moving. But he couldn't knock it in the cup. Too infuriated to worry about the penalty strokes, Barnes next tried the cleaning lady approach. Acting as if the ball were a mouse and his club a broom, he swatted at the ball while he hopped around the green. But the ball, seemingly having a mind of its own, still dodged the hole. In total frustration, Barnes even played a stroke croquet style—by standing astride the line of his putt—another violation of the rules. This exercise in masochism took all of thirty seconds before finally, mercifully, the ball plopped into the cup.

His astonished marker had frantically tried to keep score during the dervishlike performance, but he wasn't sure of the count, what with the penalty strokes and all. With total disregard for his own safety, the marker turned to the seething Barnes and said, "Well, when you catch your ass in a buzz saw, it's not too easy to tell how many teeth bit you. What did you make?"

Displaying the only self-control he had shown throughout this debacle, Barnes refrained from lunging at his playing partner's throat. Instead, he bellowed, "Twelve!" But that was only for his disastrous play on the green. Barnes actually shot a 15 for the hole.

Barnes was through with counting. In fact, he was through with the tournament, and stalked off the course, still raging mad.

J. C. Snead

1977 Tournament Players Championship

J. C. Snead discovered the hard way that a hat trick does not occur only in hockey. His hat was responsible for one of golf's craziest putts.

Snead, winner of eight Tour events, was wearing his trademark headgear—a wide-brimmed straw plantation hat—during the 1977 Tournament Players Championship at Sawgrass in Florida. Although the golfers had to battle howling winds with gusts up to fifty miles an hour, Snead still managed to keep his hat on his head for the first three holes.

On the fourth hole, Snead sent a windblown chip shot 20 feet past the cup and began walking toward the green. He was about 40 yards away when a big gust blew his panama off his head. The hat landed on its rim and began rolling like a runaway tire.

To everyone's amazement, the hat actually picked up speed and rolled up an embankment and onto the green. There, it zipped right through the legs of Snead's caddie, "Big Money" John Griffin, and kept right on rolling. Wouldn't you know that on this huge expanse of green, the hat took dead aim on Snead's ball. Snead watched incredulously as his hat bounded right into his ball, nudging it forward a few inches.

After the gallery and his playing partners roared with laughter, Snead was given some sobering news. PGA officials had to penalize him two strokes because, according to the rules, he had putted with his panama. His hat was considered part of his equipment, and any equipment that dislodges a ball calls for a penalty.

"I can't putt with my hat," Snead told the officials. But the rules said he had and the case was closed. Snead, who was leading at the time, was so rattled by the zany incident that he three-putted the hole.

"I didn't get mad about it," recalled Snead. "It was kind of disappointing, but it was just one of those funny things that happened." He earned $5,400 for finishing in a tie for thirteenth. Without the two-stroke penalty, Snead would have tied for eighth and picked up $2,750 more.

"Just think," said competitor Tom Watson. "The hat blew 40 yards before it hit his ball. How's that for luck?"

Hats incredible!

Jerry Pate

1982 World Series of Golf

No golfer who ever faced an eagle putt in a major tournament self-destructed as shamefully as Jerry Pate.

On one unforgettable hole, the 1976 U.S. Open winner learned two simple truths of golf: (1) a golfer is never safe from disaster until the ball goes in the cup, and (2) there is nowhere to hide on the green when a golfer screws up.

Unfortunately, Pate learned those lessons firsthand at one of the year's biggest tournaments—the 1982 World Series of Golf at Firestone Country Club in Akron, Ohio. "That was the stupidest hole I've ever played," he admitted. "[Playing partner] Andy Bean called me 'Bonehead' after that day."

Playing the par-5 second hole—one of the easier holes on the Firestone course—Pate reached the fringe of the green in two strokes. He lay 50 feet away from the cup, gunning for an eagle three.

Pate, relishing this golden opportunity, took an extra moment to read the green. He gave his first putt a good rap, but it rolled four feet past the hole. Pate wasn't too disappointed because he was now shooting for a very makable birdie. But again he putted too hard, and the ball skirted three feet past the hole.

Disgusted that he'd blown a chance to shave a stroke or two off his score, Pate figured that at the very least he'd make his five for par. He was wrong. His third putt lipped out. The only bright spot about his putting was that his ball was getting closer to the hole with each stroke.

Now totally exasperated and facing a bogey six, Pate got careless. With the hole between the ball and him, Pate reached over and made a backhand stab at the ball. It was one of those nonchalant tap-ins that he had successfully executed hundreds of times before. But this time the results were disastrous. The ball not only jumped over the cup but hit his foot for a two-stroke penalty. A disbelieving Pate had blown his chance for a bogey and was now lying eight. Unable to hide or make a quick getaway, Pate regrouped and finally holed out for a quadruple-bogey nine.

"I was mad when I reached over the cup to pop it in and then it hit my shoe," recalled Pate, who finished in a tie for tenth place. "For a second, I didn't know how I felt. I went from being mad to being embarrassed to laughter. It just goes to show you that in golf, it's never over until the ball is in the hole."

Jan Stephenson

1985 U.S. Women's Open

Because of one thin, little dime, Jan Stephenson lost her cool and her concentration.

Vying in the 1985 U.S. Women's Open at Baltusrol in Springfield, New Jersey, Stephenson was tied for the lead at the turn in the first round. Jan, winner of the 1983 event, brimmed with confidence and played like a winner-to-be.

But it was not to be. She was tripped up on the 11th green by a tough break when her birdie putt came up a few feet short. Jan marked her ball with a dime and stepped away, but playing partner Patty Sheehan said the mark was in her line and asked Jan to move it. Stephenson obliged. She moved her mark and then tapped it down with her putter. But when she lifted her putter, she noticed to her horror that the dime had stuck to the bottom of the club head. Before she could utter a sound, the dime fell to the green.

It happened so unexpectedly and undramatically that few in the gallery even saw it. But it was spotted by an LPGA official, who cited a USGA rule: "If, due to action by the player, accidental or otherwise, the ball marker does not remain in position, the player incurs a penalty of one stroke."

With tears welling up in her blazing eyes, Stephenson carried on a desperate but futile argument. She finally stopped squawking, but she couldn't stop fuming. "I was so mad," she said later. "The ruling proved to be extremely disruptive. I should have walked off the course."

She finished the round one stroke behind the leader, her main rival, Nancy Lopez. As she headed for the clubhouse, Jan told reporters, "I'm very upset. This never happens to Nancy Lopez."

But it has happened before—to Shirley Spork, one of the founders of the LPGA. Years ago in a tournament in Chicago, Spork marked her ball on the green with a plastic marker, tapped it down with her putter, and walked 15 feet away from the pin. When it was her turn to putt again, she couldn't find her marker. So her playing partners joined in the search. Finally, someone shouted, "Look at the bottom of your putter!" The marker was still stuck to the club head, and Spork was assessed a penalty stroke. But at least she didn't let it bother her.

Jan never recovered from her anger over the infraction and faltered throughout the rest of the tournament. "The rule was blatantly wrong," she said. "What they did to get out of it was they eventually changed the rule. It's no longer a penalty. Now you can replace the ball marker."

Dow Finsterwald

1962 Masters Tournament

A seemingly innocent practice putt ultimately cost Dow Finsterwald his only chance ever to wear the cherished green jacket as winner of the Masters.

Finsterwald, who won the 1958 PGA Championship, was playing in the first round of the 1962 Masters at Augusta National when he missed an easy two-foot putt on the fifth hole. It was something that happens to the best of them. Most players just shake it off and concentrate on the next shot. But not Finsterwald.

After tapping the ball in for a bogey, he was still perplexed over how he could have blown such a simple putt. He wondered whether he had developed a flaw in his stroke. As he started to walk toward the sixth tee, Dow stopped on the edge of the green. Totally engrossed over the missed putt, he dropped his ball on the green and then stroked it a few feet with his putter in the opposite direction of the hole. He was hoping to detect a flaw in his putting mechanics, but he didn't notice any.

Dow was suddenly jolted out of his deep thought when a tournament official informed him that he was being assessed a two-stroke penalty for practicing on the green. It was clearly against the local rules under which the Masters was being played.

Finsterwald humbly accepted the ruling without a peep of protest. "I felt very fortunate that the Masters committee only gave me a two-stroke penalty," he recalled. "They could have disqualified me. I feel they were most generous in allowing me to continue play. I have never to this day known what prompted them to do it. They certainly acted with great compassion considering there were some players who felt I should have been disqualified.

"It [practicing on the green] wasn't against the rules of golf at that time. But Augusta had put the rule in for the Masters. I was totally unaware that it was in place because I hadn't read the local rules properly.''

Although Dow may have been grateful he wasn't DQ'ed, his practice putt came back to haunt him in the Masters. After shooting a 74 (including the two-stroke penalty), Dow fired rounds of 68, 65, and 73 for a total of 280, good for a playoff berth with Arnold Palmer and Gary Player. The next day, the 18-hole playoff was won by Palmer.

But there wouldn't have been any playoff if Finsterwald hadn't been penalized. Instead, he would have won the Masters outright by two strokes.

No Ifs, Ands, or Putts About It

One of the most incredible putts never holed was that of amateur Hunter Phillips.

In 1932, Phillips, one of the best golfers at the Memphis (Tennessee) Country Club, was playing against Edward Falls in the finals of the club tournament.

Phillips came to the last hole one down and needing to make a three-foot putt to square the match and take it into extra holes. The putt wasn't a gimme, but the gallery, knowing of Phillips's golfing skill, felt certain he'd knock it in.

Phillips carefully surveyed the line from four different angles. Twice he stepped up to hit it, only to back away. Then, to the astonishment of everyone, he reached down, picked up the ball, and shook hands with his startled opponent.

"You got the match," Phillips told Falls. "There's no way I could make that thing."

BAG OF TRICKS

It's not whether you win or lose, it's how you "play" your opponent. Golfers use gamesmanship as their fifteenth club, hoping to psych out their competitors by taking their minds off the game. Sometimes, though, it gets downright ungentlemanly. For "The Sneakiest Ways of Psyching Out an Opponent," The Golf Hall of SHAME inducts the following:

Walter Hagen

The great Walter Hagen didn't win eleven national and five PGA championships on his consummate golfing skill alone. He also relied on cunning gamesmanship—of which he was the absolute master.

The crafty Sir Walter toyed with opponents' minds like yo-yos. He tricked his playing partners into using the wrong clubs. He ticked them off by taking forever to size up an easy shot. He made them squirm with offhand remarks that shattered their confidence. And he made them stew by deliberately showing up late for his starts.

If his opponents started peeking at his club selections so they could follow his lead, Hagen would con them. He once tricked Al Watrous in the 1925 PGA Championship at Olympia Fields near Chicago. The two were tied as they teed off on the 18th hole, a dangerous par-5 with water fronting the green. Although Hagen hit the longest drive, his ball landed in the rough on the left. Watrous, whose ball lay in the fairway, was away, so he had to play first. He planned to use a long iron and lay up short of the water, but then he looked over to Sir Walter, who was taking practice swings with a wood. To Watrous, that meant Hagen had a good lie and was going for the green on his second shot. Figuring that if Hagen was using a wood, so would he, Watrous replaced his iron with a wood—and drilled his shot right into the water. Hagen then smugly put away his wood and pulled out a long iron—the one he had intended to use all along. He played safely to the fairway and went on to par the hole and win the match from a duped Watrous.

The Haig often used a wrinkle on this ploy. He'd play a three-iron but take something off the hit—basically, hitting the three-iron to a five-iron distance. By hiding the "soft" shot in a big swing motion—like a baseball pitcher with a good change-up—Hagen could fool a peeker into going full bore with a three-iron and knocking the ball 20 yards past the green.

Claude Harmon, winner of the 1948 Masters, claimed Hagen sometimes played with mismarked clubs to fool those who dared eavesdrop when the Haig asked for a club from his caddie. "Hagen had a jacked-up set of irons—the four-iron was marked five, and so forth," said Harmon, "and you could get into big trouble" trying to match what club Hagen had requested.

Hagen loved to psych out opponents by strolling over and peering into their bags, then shaking his head and walking away. And on the green, he'd study their putts and then gesture that they were impossible to make.

"Make the hard shots look easy and the easy shots look hard," Sir Walter once said. He drove opponents nuts and threw off their rhythm when, at a crucial time in the match, he'd spend several long minutes studying a "difficult" shot. He once sent to the clubhouse for a folding chair so that his biggest rival, Gene Sarazen, could sit down while Hagen took his sweet time studying a simple chip shot.

Arriving late to the tee was what Hagen did best. Many old pros did that to rookies back then—without penalty of disqualification. Only Hagen did it with style.

A lover of wine, women, and song—although not necessarily in that order—Sir Walter often arrived at the golf course still wearing his tuxedo from the night before. He then leisurely changed his shoes, put on his fresh white linen knickers, and strolled to the tee.

A young Byron Nelson fell victim to this ploy at the General Brock Open at Niagara Falls. Nelson, then unknown and unsure of himself, surprised the field by leading after three rounds. On the final day, Nelson, who was to be paired with Hagen, arrived early at the tee, where he fidgeted and fretted and counted the minutes until his start. Then word came that the Haig would be late. Poor Nelson paced back and forth and took hundreds of practice swings. Two hours later Hagen finally showed up—in a white-on-white silk shirt, gold cuff links, and slicked-back hair. "Hi, boy," he said to Nelson.

"It's . . . it's a real big honor," stammered the star-struck rookie. His nerves were so frazzled from waiting that he shot a shaky 42 on the front nine, lost his lead, and finished in second place—behind Hagen.

Sir Walter's gamesmanship was at its peak during the 1919 U.S. Open at Brae Burn Country Club near Boston. Hagen and Mike Brady had tied after the final round and were set to meet in a playoff the next day.

On the evening of the playoff, Hagen and entertainer Al Jolson donned high tops and tails and squired several chorus girls to a wild party that swung until dawn. Sometime during the night, a well-meaning friend told Hagen, "For God's sake, Walter, why don't you go to bed and get some sleep so you'll be in shape for the playoff tomorrow. You can be sure that Mike has been in bed and been sleeping for hours." Hagen laughed and said, "He may be in bed, right enough, but he ain't sleeping any more than I am."

The only sleep Hagen caught was a catnap while being driven to the course where, still decked out in white tie and tails, he arrived late, as usual. While officials gave Hagen time to change into his clothes, a frustrated Brady cooled his heels and learned about Hagen's cocky remark from the previous night.

So he tried to give Hagen a dose of his own medicine. On the first tee, Brady made a big production of rolling up his sleeves and spitting on his hands before teeing off. But Hagen got even. On the second hole, he sidled up to Brady and whispered, "Mike, you oughta roll those sleeves back down. You're letting everyone see how the muscles in your forearms are quivering. It's a dead giveaway." Brady then hit his tee shot into the woods bordering the fairway and wound up with a double-bogey six. Hagen won the championship by a stroke.

Lew (The Chin) Worsham

1947 U.S. Open

It took some sneaky gamesmanship by Lew (The Chin) Worsham to steal the 1947 U.S. Open championship from Sam Snead.

"I hold no grudge against Lew," said Snead, winner of 84 Tour events. "He did what he needed to do if he was to win. And if a man can't defend himself against a smart psychologist, he belongs in the clubhouse playing gin and not out there with the big-time cutthroats."

Although Snead eventually fell victim to two Worsham psych jobs, he certainly didn't belong in the clubhouse; not after he forced a playoff with the Chin by making a clutch 20-foot downhill putt on the 72nd hole.

In the 18-hole playoff at the St. Louis Country Club, Snead held a one-stroke lead as he prepared to chip from 12 feet away onto the 17th green. Suddenly he became aware of loud, heavy breathing. It was coming from Worsham, who had just climbed a hill to the green and now stood a few feet away.

"You better move back a little, Chin," said Snead. "Just give me a little more room." Worsham moved away as Snead tried to regain his concentration. Then he hit a weak chip that left a six-foot putt for par. Snead missed his putt for a bogey, but Worsham made his par, squaring the match as they entered the final hole.

Recalled Snead, "One reason my chip wasn't better, I'll swear, was that I was upset by Worsham's wheezing, and I wasn't a hundred percent concentrated on the shot."

Both reached the 18th green in two. Worsham putted first from 30 feet, leaving the ball shy about three feet from the hole. Snead then left his putt short, about the same distance away.

Seeing that Worsham was holding his ball, having marked it with a coin, Snead lined up his putt for par. Just as Snead was set to putt, Worsham suddenly stepped in front of him and said, "Wait a minute. What are you doing?"

"I'm putting out," replied Snead, annoyed by the Chin's seeming breach of etiquette.

"Well, maybe not," said Worsham. "Are you sure you're away? I think maybe I am and have the first shot." He knew that whoever putted first had an advantage. If he holed out, pressure on his opponent would greatly increase. So Worsham asked USGA official Ike Grainger for a measurement.

Grainger used a tape measure to find Snead 30½ inches from the cup and Worsham 30 inches away. The damage had been done, though; Snead's concentration had been broken. Annoyed by the five-minute interruption, Snead missed his putt. Worsham then calmly sank his and claimed the U.S. Open title.

"I'll always believe I'd have won this Open if the two interruptions of my thinking hadn't happened," Snead said.

The wily Worsham later said that his actions on the last two holes "have been described by some as a breach of etiquette, by others as gamesmanship on my part. All I can say is I have many fond memories of St. Louis in 1947."

Jerry McGee

1967 Milwaukee Open

As a rookie, Jerry McGee pulled the old "paralysis by analysis" scam on a veteran—but only after Jerry was bamboozled by a similar con job.

The young McGee, who would become a four-time winner on the PGA Tour, had shot a 68 in the first round of the 1967 Milwaukee Open at Northshore Country Club. The veteran, whom McGee now refuses to name, finished the day with a 73. According to McGee, here's what happened next:

"After the round, I went to the practice range, where I was hitting drive after drive," McGee recalled. "Every shot was perfect. I was deep in concentration, popping ball after ball at the 250-yard marker. Then I realized that somebody was watching me. I turned around and it was the old pro, sitting on his bag right behind me.''

McGee was surprised that a veteran and winner of several Tour events would be studying the swing of a rookie.

"Rook," said the pro, "that was a super round you played today. But I have to be honest with you. I just can't believe you shot a 68 with that grip." The crafty veteran then left without uttering another word.

Up until then McGee had never even thought twice about his grip. But suddenly he couldn't hit a ball straight. All he could think about was his grip. He dwelled on it on the practice tee, then in bed that night, and again the next morning warming up.

McGee started the second round with two double-bogeys and another bogey while the old pro parred the first three holes. Not until they reached the fourth tee did it dawn on McGee that the veteran had pulled a psych job on him. With the mettle of a more seasoned player, McGee decided to turn the tables and put a sting on the perpetrator.

McGee strolled up to him and, with a voice dripping in reverence, said, "You know, I've really got a lot of respect for you. Do you mind if I ask you a question?"

"Why sure, rook, ask me anything you want," said the smiling pro, obviously delighted that the seed he had planted in McGee's mind had sprouted and messed up his game.

"Well, I'm really trying to work on my grip, trying to make it as good as yours," said McGee. "But I've got to ask you," he added, putting on his best impersonation of wide-eyed innocence, "do you inhale or exhale at impact?"

The old pro looked quizzically at McGee and stammered, "Well, uh, I don't know." For the rest of the round the veteran hit it all over the place. After he putted out, the old pro, his face flushed with anger, stormed over to McGee, jabbed a finger in his chest, and snarled, "You little SOB, you got back at me!"

Frank Stranahan and Smiley Quick
1946 Western Amateur

In one of the most shameful exhibitions of mean-spirited gamesmanship ever displayed in a championship match, Frank Stranahan and Smiley Quick tried to beat each other with insults and threats instead of woods and irons.

If words had been fists, their match would have been a barroom brawl. Golfing etiquette went the way of the feathery and gutty.

The two tournament golfers were destined to clash; they came from opposite sides of the fairway. Stranahan, twenty-four, the son of a multimillionaire and winner of several amateur titles, would go on to win the British Amateur in 1948 and 1950. He was a clean-living health-food nut who played for medals, not money, since his father picked up the tab. Frank's broad shoulders, good looks, and chestnut hair made him the idol of the bobby-sox brigade. In contrast, the gritty, leather-tough thirty-nine-year-old Quick was a former caddie and trapeze artist who had to struggle for everything he got. Before turning pro in 1948, he survived by hustling fat cats on the golf course. The short, musclebound Smiley, the 1946 Amateur Public Links champion, developed a vigorous playing style that matched his cocky, colorful personality.

Despite their differences, the two golfers possessed many similar traits—a burning desire to win, a huge ego, a quick temper, and a vicious tongue. Ironically, it was their similarities that triggered hostilities unprecedented in championship golf.

Their bitter battle unfolded when the two played against each other in the 1946 Western Amateur in Duluth, Minnesota. Smiley began giving Frank the "treatment," figuring that his pampered rival wouldn't know how to meet the challenge. At first it was hard-edged ribbing as Quick entertained the spectators with dire predictions of Stranahan's fate: "Watch him hit it right into the bunker," or, "He couldn't make that putt if he dug a trench to the hole."

But Frank dished it right back: "He talks when he's scared," and, "The only thing he knows how to swing is a trapeze."

Soon words weren't enough. On the green, they rudely stood in the lines of each other's putts, moved about just as the other was putting, or jingled change in their pockets. Once, Stranahan putted out and arrogantly strolled on to the next tee, leaving Smiley to putt out alone. Whenever Frank hit into the rough, Quick followed him and watched as if he suspected Stranahan would try to improve his lie. This rancor and vitriol lasted throughout the entire 36-hole match and into a sudden-death playoff.

"All your millions won't help you now," Smiley growled at Frank as they teed off on the 37th hole. "I'm going to put the spurs to you now."

"With what?" snapped Stranahan.

"It won't take much with that sissy swing you've got," retorted Smiley.

At the 39th hole, Quick's antagonism turned even more hostile when he threatened Stranahan by saying, "I'm going to end this match now. Then I'm going to take care of you out behind the clubhouse."

Frank didn't say a word. He let his putter answer by sinking a 12-footer for a birdie to win the overtime match. Smiley was anything but that as he walked over, halfheartedly shook Frank's hand and disappeared. Thus ended the war of the words.

Up a Tree

Slammin' Sammy Snead was playing a practice round before the 1967 Masters when the old veteran made a $5 Nassau bet with South African rookie Bobby Cole, the 1966 British Amateur champion.

They were tied when they reached the tee at Augusta National's famous 13th hole, a par-5 with a slight dogleg to the left guarded by pine trees and Rae's Creek. The fifty-five-year-old Snead turned to the twenty-year-old Cole and said, "Bobby, when I was your age, I could knock the ball over those pine trees."

Bobby took the remark as a challenge, teed it up, and boldly tried to carry the trees. But his ball was gobbled up by the pines. "Man," said Bobby, "I can't hit the ball over those trees. How did you do it?"

Snead gave a sly smile and said, "Bobby, when I was your age, those trees were only twenty feet tall." Snead went on to win the Nassau.

Letter-Perfect Scam

Before a big match between Walter Hagen and Gene Sarazen at the Westchester-Biltmore in 1922, Sarazen received an orange tie enclosed with a fan letter from a Ziegfeld show girl who said she desperately wanted him to beat the Haig.

"Don't look for me in the gallery," said the note. "I don't want you to take your mind off Hagen. I want you to wear this tie for good luck."

On the day of the match, Sarazen donned the tie, and every chance he got, he scoped the gallery for the show girl. "It was raining and the colors of the tie ran all over my shirt and I was a mess," Sarazen recalled. "Not only that, but I spent a lot of time looking around for that girl and I lost my concentration."

During a break at the turn, Hagen told Sarazen, "Say, that's a handsome tie you've got on. Where'd you get it?"

"A friend," Sarazen replied.

"Is this friend your mysterious admirer, a Follies girl who wanted you to pay strict attention to beating me?"

"Why, yes," said Sarazen. "How did you know?" But one look at Hagen's grinning face and Sarazen knew the letter had been written by none other than the Haig himself.

WAY OFF COURSE

*Some courses are so horrifying that your clubs get anxiety attacks.
The links play as though they were designed by Jason as a backdrop
to a* Friday the 13th *movie. Then there are the wacky courses where
you expect to see Pee Wee Herman as the starter. For "The Most
Outrageous Golf Courses in the World," The Golf Hall of SHAME
inducts the following:*

Yellowknife Golf Club

Yellowknife, Northwest Territories, Canada

Yellowknife Golf Club has driven hundreds of golfers stark "raven"
mad—because eagle-sized ravens swoop down from the trees and snatch
golf balls right off the fairways.

It's the only course in the world where birdies get their golfers about
as often as golfers get their birdies.

It's also the northernmost course in the world, located just 250 miles
south of the Arctic Circle.

Aside from its high(flying) crime rate, the nine-hole, par-36 Yellowknife
plays like one big bunker. That's because the entire course is all sand.
Even the greens are sand. Spread out among rocks and evergreens,
Yellowknife is like a Canadian wilderness preserve with flagsticks. What
little grass sprouts through the sandy fairways is called a hazard. As a
matter of fact, when a ball lands in one of the few weed patches, golfers
say they've hit into a "green trap."

The grueling conditions make a round here an exercise in survival.
Golfers must also deal with squadrons of voracious mosquitoes and
tenacious black flies.

But you don't hear golfers grumbling about the green traps, the sandy fairways, or the swarming insects. No, they're peeved about those damned ravens.

For some Hitchcockian or Poe-etic reason, the ravens at Yellowknife have been stealing golf balls—especially new, shiny, white ones—since 1950. The modus operandi is always the same. A raven usually perches on a tree about 200 yards away from a tee and waits for a drive to land. Then, ignoring the angry shouts of the golfer, the bird glides down to the ball, picks it up in its beak, and heads off to its stash.

The thefts have led to the adoption of a local rule. On the back of every Yellowknife scorecard, Rule No. 6 states, "No penalty assessed when ball carried off by raven."

Years ago golfers brought along .22-caliber rifles or shotguns to scare or kill the ravens. But, according to accounts back then, the ladies of the community got up in a different sort of arms and demanded an immediate end to the sniping. They argued that ravens were the only birds remaining in the desolate area during long winter months, and the women were happy for *any* living company they could get.

Few of the birds were ever killed. "The ravens were either very cunning or our golfers were extremely poor shots," said longtime golfer George Inglis. "I've seen only one dead raven on the course. Someone had hung him from a fairway tree, possibly in an attempt to show the other ravens that crime doesn't pay."

But there has been no letup of these foul deeds. In fact, the winged theft ring has become even bolder. On several occasions, a golfer has been robbed by the ravens of as many as *six* balls in a single round, according to club official Ed Cook.

There are two schools of thought about the ravens' motives: (1) The birds are stupid. They believe the balls are eggs and cart them off to their nests or roosting areas. (2) The birds hate golfers. That may explain why many ravens simply bury the balls in the sand elsewhere on the course.

In recent years, however, some ravens have been hiding their booty far from the course. Three miles away, hikers found a raven's nest crammed with 78 balls. "It seems a new game has developed between ravens to see which can steal the most balls," said Cook. "Within one week, two caches of balls were found on roofs of buildings in [the town of] Yellowknife. More than fifty were found on one roof, and on another high-rise building there were more than a hundred!"

It was suggested by one victimized golfer that members of Yellowknife once again be allowed to carry a fifteenth club in their bags—the trusty shotgun. What then would happen to all the ball thieving? Quoth the raven, "Nevermore."

Municipal Golf Courses

New York City

They called it urban guerrilla golf.

It was a dangerous game played by those courageous—and foolish—enough to golf on any of New York's 13 municipal courses during the 1970s, when the links were as lawless as the wild west. Golfers encountered rather unique hazards—like muggers, abandoned cars, and dead bodies.

"You were considered to have had a good game if you could make it around the course without getting robbed or hassled by thugs," said golfer Jeff Feldman. "Even then, if you made it safely, there was still the chance that your car was ripped off from the parking lot."

At the Pelham Golf Course, golfer Don Jerome complained to *The New York Times* that one of his tee shots bounced into an abandoned car *on the fairway*, costing him a stroke. A friend of his was robbed while lining up an approach shot, costing him $65 and his credit cards. "Something like that disrupts a golfer's concentration," said Jerome in a classic Big Apple understatement.

To combat the muggers, several golfers played with guard dogs by their sides. Some carried cans of Mace in their bags, while still others went so far as to pack pistols. Instead of playing in twosomes or foursomes, they played in eightsomes or even sixteensomes for added protection.

It wasn't uncommon for an early-bird golfer to come upon a corpse. "We get a certain number of dead bodies," John DeMatteo, a course supervisor, told *The Times* in 1985. "I try not to be the first one out on the course in the morning."

The number of bodies that golfers had to sidestep didn't come close to matching the number of discarded appliances, dumped trash, and abandoned cars that littered the courses. Stolen cars driven onto the courses at night by punks were left stuck in sand traps.

Golf carts were easy targets for young gang members. They'd run out of the bushes and swipe carts while players were putting. In 1985, a gang broke into the cart barn at Clearview in Queens and played demolition derby with about 25 carts. Another of the gang's pastimes was driving stolen carts onto the expressway to their Queens neighborhood.

Golfers were constantly trying to compete with nonplayers for use of the links. With so few open spaces in the city, the golf courses were used as soccer fields, picnic areas, dirt-bike paths, lovers' lanes, and even battlefields for gangs. "They stopped a gang fight once to let us play through," golfer Jane Angelo told *The Times*.

Just getting to the first tee was a test of stamina, nerves, and fists. "Man, we'd have to line up in the middle of the night, like three or four in the morning, just so we'd be able to get on the course when it opened," said golfer Jim Toon. "Somebody would try to sneak in ahead of you, and if you mouthed off at him, you'd get your block knocked off—unless you were bigger than he was. Then you had to deal with the cheap clowns who would sneak onto the course at about the third or fourth hole. They knew nothing was going to happen to them. Who was going to stop them?"

Eventually the city brought in private companies to manage the courses. These firms replaced the war-zone mentality with a country-club atmosphere and made the courses safe and fun again for golfers.

Despite dramatic improvements, some problems, like a chronic hook, still persist. "We've gone from abandoned cars to abandoned limousines," said Arnie Muniz, general manager of the Pelham Golf Course. "Over New Years [1989], someone stole a limo and left it on the course. Well, at least we're moving up in the world."

Elephant Hills Country Club
Victoria Falls, Zimbabwe, Africa

Playing golf at Elephant Hills Country Club was no sweat—if you were Tarzan.

The course was so junglelike, you felt like swinging from vines rather than from tees. For every hazard you could carry, there was one—namely buffalo or waterbuck—that could carry you. Here, your golf balls didn't bite the greens as often as crocodiles did.

The site of the 18-hole course, which was designed by Gary Player and built in 1975, seemed more suited for big-game hunters than golfers. Situated among the baobab and mopani trees near the banks of the Zambezi River, the course was the home of elephants, hippopotami, leopards, lions, and warthogs, who didn't fully appreciate the sport. And they let golfers know it. While man played golf, beast played havoc.

"It was touch and go when an irate hippo charged me near the green of the fourth hole," recalled Mike Riddle, course superintendent. "He only just missed me.

"Warthogs were the real swine. They were always digging holes in the fairways. We once spent $2,000 in just three months to repair the holes." Despite a two-strand wire fence, hippos sank their bellies on the greens, leaving huge depressions. Elephants also left their mark on the greens— large impressions from their feet.

At tournament time, sudden death took on an ominous new meaning. Players were forced to keep a wary eye out for death-dealing snakes known as puff adders; African ants with a hungry appetite for flesh; and Charlie the crocodile, who would leave his water hazard home at the eighth hole to roam the course. The scariest moment for club member

Dr. Vane Vincent happened one day on the back nine when he nearly tripped over a pair of dozing leopards. He broke into a sprint in one direction while, fortunately, the equally startled leopards fled in the opposite direction.

Not every animal was life-threatening. There were times when a wild baboon would dart out from the dark, thick rough, pick up an errant shot, and gleefully flee with the ball.

The course's local rules reflected the uneasy relationship between man and beast. For example:

- If a player is chased by an elephant, "he shall be allowed to return to his ball, which shall be played as it lies, whether or not the animal had trodden thereon."
- "If a player's ball lands in the droppings of an animal, such a ball may be cleaned and dropped within two club-lengths, without penalty."
- If a ball comes to rest within a tail's distance of a sleeping buffalo, "it may be removed and dropped no nearer the hole without penalty. More than a tail length, the ball shall be played as it lies."
- If a player's ball hits a running warthog (which runs with its tail pointed straight up), this "does not entitle the player to replay the shot, except when the ball strikes the tail, in which case it shall be deemed to have struck a miniature moving flagpole."

Before joining the PGA Tour, Nick Price, of Zimbabwe, once hit a warthog just below its "miniature moving flagpole" at Elephant Hills. Recalled Price, "On the first tee, I pulled my drive and hit a warthog on his behind. The hog was less than a hundred yards from the tee, and the ball was traveling so fast that it toppled the hog over. He got up and ran into the bushes. He actually saved me a stroke or two because he kept the ball in play."

What finally brought an end to Elephant Hills was the world's most dangerous animal—man. When civil war broke out in 1977, the country club and course were destroyed by rocket fire. Today the fairways, tees, and greens are once again the sole domain of buffalo, waterbuck, warthogs, vervet monkeys, lions, and leopards.

Laurens Golf and Country Club

Laurens, Iowa

At the Laurens Golf and Country Club, golfers are warned that before hitting, they look both ways—and up. For good reason. Incredibly, the golf course doubles as an airport.

No links in the world has more championship flights than the zany one in Laurens, Iowa, a small town of 1,600 people. The local airport's single

grass runway cuts through the rough and fairways on seven of the nine holes. As a result, golfers must dodge the crop dusters and small single-engine planes that touch down on the 1,200-foot-long runway.

"The planes have the right of way," says Norman Hartsock, a commercial spray pilot. "There are times when the golfers don't see me coming down the runway. They turn around and their eyes get as big as basketballs. They sure do run."

A pilot landing at Laurens usually circles the course first and then buzzes once to warn golfers that he is about to land. But out-of-town golfers, in particular, have been known to miss the message.

"The local people generally know how to get out of the way when a plane circles over, but sometimes the guests don't know that the rough is a runway," said Ronald Harms, a local dentist and golfer. "They just gawk and wave as a plane gets closer and closer to them. Sooner or later they run out of the way. After landing, the pilot usually gets out of his plane screaming and mad as the dickens."

Sometimes golfers haven't been too thrilled over halting their game to allow a crop duster to play through. "There have been a few instances where golfers resent the planes," said Hartsock. "Pilots have been ready to land only to see that the golfers had left their golf carts right in the middle of the runway."

The course was first laid out in the late 1950s, several years after some private pilots had built the grass runway for their own use. Eventually the pilots agreed to lease the land for the links, with the understanding that they could still land their planes on the runway.

Pilot Glen Siddall said the bizarre arrangement has worked fairly well. But he did admit that some mean-spirited golfers have smashed the runway lights with their clubs, out of either frustration over a bad game or irritation over the planes. "If some of the golfers are stubborn and don't move, then the planes just buzz them and scare them," he said. "They've all got electric carts, and it's really something to fly down low and see them scatter."

So far, there have been no accidents involving golfers and pilots, said Siddall. However, one flier misplayed the course. "The pilot was coming in at night and his wife was supposed to be there waiting for him with her car lights on," recalled Siddall. "But she didn't show up. He couldn't see, and he misjudged the runway and landed on the green."

War Courses

Richmond Golf Club, England, 1940
Yankee Bee Country Club, South Pacific, 1943
Saigon Country Club, South Vietnam, 1966

Hundreds of golfers were so insanely addicted to the game that they risked life and limb to play on courses situated smack dab in the middle of raging war zones. Every time these foolhardy linksmen teed up, they were never quite sure whether or not they would finish the round alive. But as one brash Englishman who played golf throughout World War II declared, "What a way to go!"

In 1940, members of the Richmond Golf Club in England weren't going to let the bombing of Britain stop them from playing their favorite sport. Of course, there were a few "temporary rules" that they had to observe. For example:

- "The positions of known delayed-action bombs are marked by red flags at a reasonably, but not guaranteed, safe distance from the bombs."
- "A ball moved by enemy action may be replaced as near as possible to where it lay, or if lost or destroyed, a ball may be dropped not nearer the hole without penalty."
- "A player whose stroke is affected by the simultaneous explosion of a bomb or shell, or by machine-gun fire, may play another ball from the same place. Penalty one stroke."

Members were also asked to pick up any bomb and shrapnel splinters that they spotted on the course to avoid damage to the mowing machines.

At the height of World War II, in 1943, members of a U.S. Navy Sea Bee construction unit were such golf nuts that they hacked out a nine-hole golf course from the jungle of a South Pacific island—between bombings by the Japanese.

Every available man volunteered to clear a space on the island for what was to be known as the Yankee Bee Country Club. They filled in foxholes and bomb craters and placed sawdust traps throughout the fairways and around the clover greens. Meanwhile, the Japanese air force created several new unplanned bunkers with each bombing raid.

The Sea Bees handmade their clubs out of various tools. The heads were hammered and shaped from chisels, hatchet heads, and pieces of iron, while the shafts were cut and sanded from axe-pick handles.

Golf balls were guarded more carefully than ammo because the club possessed only four balls—all old and battered. In fact, the balls were so prized that the penalty for losing one was not a stroke or two, but one month's suspension from play. Remarkably, no one ever lost a ball.

When the course opened, grass seemed to grow overnight, making the greens much too shaggy. Since the Sea Bees had no lawn mower, they used the next best thing—a goat. It took the promise of a little extra chow to make a Marine sergeant hand over his pet three-month-old goat, Jimmy. The goat, who was given the rank of CGK (Chief Greens Keeper), kept the course well-trimmed. However, he ate grass everywhere except where he was needed most. So he had to be tied with a 50-foot rope to the area in need of trimming. That way, a different part of the course was mowed each day. Golfers knew they should never knock a ball in Jimmy's direction because, like all goats, he ate everything in sight.

For the first club championship, 45 servicemen paid a 50-cent entry fee. "Nothing could compare with the tournament put on by the Yankee Bee's jungle course," wrote Marine Corps combat correspondent Sergeant Ralph Peck. "Stateside tournaments find the gallery heading for the clubhouse at the outbreak of a rainstorm. Here, an occasional bombing from the Japs adds to the many hazards, sending players and spectators scampering into the many foxholes nestled about the course." The winner won a 16-inch trophy hammered from an empty 105mm shell and adorned with two .50-caliber shells.

That same sense of audacity spurred American servicemen to play golf at the dangerous Saigon Country Club during the Vietnam War.

"There was the constant possibility that a sniper might zap you as you lined up your putt," wrote freelance writer Henry Billings, who back then was an Army Intelligence officer at Tan Son Nhut Air Base. "There was also the clear and present chance that a stray mortar round might give you a much larger cup as your target."

Billings and other GI's who played golf at the Saigon Country Club in their free time knew that a blast from the bunker could be either an explosive golf shot or just an explosive. They were constantly on the alert for terrorists. Sand traps had to be checked for booby traps set by the Viet Cong, and ball washers had to be examined to make sure they weren't rigged with plastic explosives.

"I thought about that often when I first arrived," said Billings. "But after a while I worried more about my short-iron game—which was awful—than a random terrorist attack."

About the only good feature of the 18-hole course was that it was nearly impossible to lose a ball. A platoon of Vietnamese youngsters scoured the roughs for balls and resold them to the players. "Sometimes the youngsters were not satisfied with honest labor," Billings recalled. "They would hide in the bushes about 200 yards down range and pounce on the ball when it landed. On a par-5, I spanked a sweet three-wood shot that came down in front of the green and rolled to within three feet of the hole. Eagle city. Before I could shout for joy, a barefoot urchin dashed onto the green and made off with my ball. My playing companion, standing less than ten feet from me, claimed that he had not seen the shot and that the only fair thing to do would be for me to hit again—and he generously agreed to assess no penalty for a lost ball. I holed out in eight."

El Morro Golf Course

San Juan, Puerto Rico

You couldn't just play the El Morro Golf Course; you had to attack it—with machine guns, mortars, and grenades. Even then, you'd lose.

No one has ever beaten El Morro . . . and no one ever will. That's because the course, which existed from 1915 to 1965, was actually part of an embattled centuries-old fortress built by the Spanish conquistadores in 1539 to overlook and guard the harbor at San Juan, Puerto Rico.

El Morro golfers considered it appropriate that the conquistadores were experts in torture. This zany nine-hole course snaked its way through ramparts, towers, moats, bridges, stockades, entrenchments, bunkers, and parapets.

Three of the holes were played within the dry moats of the fort, which included a dogleg to the right. Getting to the cup usually required carom shots off the 30-foot-high sandstone and stucco walls. The best scores on the course were made not by the best golfers, but by the best billiard players.

The golfers also had to deal with the trade winds, which whistle in off the Atlantic and average gusts of 40 miles per hour, ruining otherwise perfect shots. The 126-yard third hole (shown in photo) was a special horror. Golfers had to tee off from a high rampart into a stiff crosswind, down through an arched stone bridge to the green, in a dry moat only 15 yards wide. On another hole, a slice sent the ball plunging 50 feet below into the bay; a hook sent the ball over another wall, down into a cemetery.

Because the course was so small, on crowded weekends the cry of "Fore!" often caused as many as a dozen golfers to hit the dirt at the same time. Balls came careening across the course from all directions, bouncing off stone bunkers, bulwarks, and parapets. Caddies actually wore steel combat helmets to protect themselves.

34

The course traced its beginnings back to 1902, when American soldiers stationed at Fort Brooke made a base out of the fortress, known officially as Castillo San Felipe del Morro. When they were off duty, some of the soldiers started hitting golf balls around the parade ground. By World War I, the full 2,467-yard layout was completed and used solely by military personnel and their guests.

"It's the only fort in the world that was bombarded with golf balls instead of bombs," said Ron Gibbs, curator of El Morro, now part of the national park system. "Visitors can see pockmarks all over the sandstone and stucco walls. Some people think those holes are from battles; they're really imprints from golf balls. It must have been one real tough course."

Courses Where You Have a Legitimate Excuse for Blowing a Shot

Golf Club of Lebanon, Beirut, Lebanon: Members must tee off behind huge red earthen mounds (see photo on next page). These mounds were built up to stop bullets and shrapnel from the fighting that has raged around the course for years. Two pounds of bullets were picked up on the

UPI/BETTMANN NEWSPHOTOS

course after one particularly heavy skirmish. "But it's worth it," said club president Salim Salam. "Golf's about the only recreation that's left around here."

Jinja Golf Course, Uganda, Africa: Golfers must learn a few unsettling local rules when playing here. For example, "If a ball comes to rest in dangerous proximity to a crocodile, another ball may be dropped." Or, "Elephants have the right of way." Also, a golf ball may be lifted from the footprint of a hippopotamus and dropped without penalty.

Francis Brown Golf Course, Mauna Lani Bay, Hawaii: A curse rides on the lava-rock-and-water-ringed 199-yard par-3 sixth hole in which golfers must send their tee shots over an inlet. Golfers who score a bogey or worse and swipe a piece of lava rock are doomed to repeat their score from this hole on every par-3 they play the remainder of their golf lives.

Mathura Golf Course, Mathura, India: On the 14th hole—known as the "Temple Tee" because there is a hallowed temple in the middle of the 542-yard fairway—golfers are expected to play over the temple's dome.

To do otherwise, golfers risk some unnamed horrible "penalty"—one that is decided by the temple's deity.

Glen Canyon Golf Course, Page, Arizona: The local rule is guaranteed to keep golfers' eyes glued to the ground: "If your ball lands within a club's length of a rattlesnake, you are allowed to move the ball."

Jasper Park Lodge Golf Course, Alberta, Canada: Golfers are urged to approach greens with extreme caution. Those soft, cushiony putting surfaces are comfy spots for bears to soak up a few rays after a long winter's nap. The course became so unbearable that a collie named Wolf was recruited to drive the furry beasts away.

Port Sudan Country Club, Sudan, Africa: Golfers must yield the right of way to camel trains that slowly make their way across this desert golf course. It has prompted a local rule that states: "Balls may be removed from camel skeletons or cactus and replaced on the course NO NEARER THE HOLE!"

The Horrors of Pebble Beach

On the Rebound
Henry Ransom, a veteran pro from Texas, ran into trouble at Cypress Point, on the infamous 16th hole. His drive faded, hit the cliff below the green, and fell to the beach.

Three times he wedged shots near the top of the cliff and three times the ball rolled back down. On his next shot, the ball ricocheted back off the rocks—and struck him right in the stomach. Ransom then ordered his caddie to pick up the ball and angrily stalked off, muttering, "When the hole starts hitting back at me, it's time to quit!"

16 Is the Wrong Number
Until Hans Merrell's disastrous 19, veteran touring pro Porky Oliver held the Cypress Point course record for the worst score on one hole—he swatted a pitiful 16 on the dreaded 16th hole in the 1953 Crosby.

After drilling five shots into the ocean, Porky carried the water, only to land into tangled ice plant with its fleshy spikelike leaves. He chopped around in the foliage until finally holing out with his unsweet 16. Word spread fast, and when Porky finished, there was a message waiting for him in the clubhouse: "Porky Oliver, please call long-distance operator . . . number 16."

The Secret Word Is Quit
It was on Cypress Point's cursed 16th hole that Groucho Marx gave up golf forever.

Playing against TV host Ed Sullivan, Groucho, who never broke 90, smacked five straight tee shots into the blue Pacific. After many years of golfing frustrations, he had learned to control his temper, so he very calmly picked up his club-laden bag, walked over to the edge of the cliff, and tossed the bag into the ocean.

"It's not that I'm a poor loser," Groucho said later, "but I figured if I couldn't beat a fellow who has no neck, I've got to be the world's worst golfer and I have no right to be on a course at all."

Through the Grace of God

Perhaps no incident better symbolizes the fickleness that has made Pebble Beach so vexing for less-than-perfect golfers than what happened to Matt Palacio.

In the 1965 Crosby, the San Francisco amateur hit his drive on the seaside 18th in the general direction of Japan and muttered, "Only God can save that one."

Just then the waves receded. The ball struck a bare rock and miraculously caromed back onto a favorable spot on the fairway.

Palacio gazed up to the heavens and shouted, "Thank you, God!"

No Bones About It, This Course Was Creepy

In 1937, Walter Hagen joined fellow golfer and trick-shot artist Joe Kirkwood on a global tour where they played on some of the strangest courses in the world.

Among the most bizarre was a course laid out over a sacred burial ground outside Shanghai, China. The curious custom of interring the bodies on the surface of the ground and then covering them with soil created plenty of natural traps and bunkers.

Kirkwood was a trifle unnerved on the 18th hole when his tee shot strayed from the fairway and landed on a burial mound. As Kirkwood prepared to hit a five-iron second shot to the green, Hagen kidded him by saying, "Don't take too much divot, Joe. A hand might be extended to you from the mound."

Kirkwood shuddered at the thought. Then he really freaked out after his shot. He looked down at his divot and saw an elbow sticking up from the soil!

THE FLUB CLUB

On the course, golfers must make as many decisions as the CEO of a Fortune 500 company. Unfortunately, many linksmen make the wrong choices and bankrupt their game. For "The Costliest Decisions Ever Made by Players," The Golf Hall of SHAME inducts the following:

Al Watrous

1932 PGA Championship

Al Watrous felt so sorry for his opponent that he decided to concede him a putt. But before long Watrous felt sorry he ever did it.

He chose to violate an unwritten rule in golf—never give consolation to the enemy. His compassionate decision backfired at the 1932 PGA Championship on the Keller Course in St. Paul, Minnesota, during a 36-hole match against Scotsman Bobby Cruickshank.

Watrous, winner of 34 tournaments, had built a huge, seemingly insurmountable lead—nine up with only 13 holes to play. On the par-3 sixth hole, the devastated Cruickshank resignedly conceded Watrous's short three-foot putt for par. After surveying his own six-footer that he needed for par, Cruickshank turned to Watrous and lamented, "This is the worst beating I've ever had."

The words seemed to soften Watrous's competitive backbone. Sure, he wanted to win, but he didn't want to humiliate a fellow professional competitor. Recalled Watrous, "I would be going ten up if he missed the putt. Feeling a bit sorry for him and not wanting to see him go down in double figures, I conceded him the putt.

"I can remember so clearly that as we walked off the green to the next tee, we passed a man who had observed the play and the conceded putt. As I went by him, I heard him say to another spectator, 'He shouldn't have done that! He might be sorry for that!' "

Watrous didn't think much of the comment until Cruickshank won the next three holes with a birdie and two pars. "I still remember the change in attitude of both of us as we went to the tenth tee," recalled Watrous, the longtime pro at Oakland Hills Country Club near Detroit. "Earlier we had been discussing Bobby's chances of getting a job [as a golf pro] at one of the Detroit courses and how I could help him. Suddenly, Bobby was all business. The friendliness went out the window. He could sense that he was back in the match."

Watrous played well, but Cruickshank played brilliantly, dazzling the gallery with spectacular putting. On 12 straight holes after the famous conceded putt, Cruickshank had an amazing nine one-putts. One of them was a 70-footer on the 15th hole. Shooting six-under on the back nine, he knocked in another long putt for a birdie at 18 to force a sudden-death playoff.

Watrous tried hard to forget that conceded putt as they halved the first three overtime holes. On the 140-yard par-3 fourth hole, it looked like his nice-guy blunder would not cost him the championship after all. Cruickshank took a bogey four while Watrous, who placed his tee shot just two feet from the hole, hadn't even made his second stroke.

Cruickshank started to shake hands with Watrous but figured he'd wait until Watrous made the putt. But Watrous's delicate downhill putt skipped past the hole and stopped not more than a foot away. It looked like a simple tap-in. Watrous thought Cruickshank would graciously concede the putt, but the Scot was not about to do any such thing—not after he'd seen what a tremendous impact that conceded sixth-hole putt had on him. Then, to the gasps of the gallery, Watrous's easy one-foot putt skirted the cup. Unbelievably, Watrous had three-putted from two feet away. Both golfers halved the hole in bogey fours.

On the next hole Watrous was so rattled that he blew a three-foot putt that would have tied Cruickshank, who holed a six-footer for par and an incredible come-from-behind win.

What did Watrous learn from this match? "Don't ever concede your opponent a putt—not even a two-incher!"

Phil Rodgers

1962 U.S. Open

For Phil Rodgers, the tree of knowledge was a pine on whose branch his ball had landed. And what he learned was that he shouldn't have tried to hit his ball out of the tree.

Rather than take a penalty drop, Rodgers swiped at the ball four times—just enough to cost him the 1962 U.S. Open.

In the first round at the Oakmont (Pennsylvania) Country Club, Rodgers, winner of the 1962 Los Angeles and Tucson Opens, was two under par when he reached the 292-yard par-4 dogleg 17th hole. It was here that he made two fatal decisions. "I tried to cut the corner on my tee shot and carry the pine trees," he recalled. "My shot hit a pine tree. But I had no idea it was going to stay there."

His ball nestled in the tree like a roosting swallow, about four feet off the ground. The ball didn't even flutter. It just lay there mockingly on a branch.

"My ball was sitting very precariously in there," Rodgers said. "It didn't look like it would take any effort at all to fall. If you touched it or blew on it, the ball would have probably fallen."

Rodgers had another decision to make: either declare it an unplayable lie and take a one-stroke penalty and a drop; or try to gouge it out of there. "It was a six-foot star pine, sort of like a Christmas tree with rows of branches, and my ball was stuck on about the fifth floor," he said. "So I decided to try to knock it out."

Swinging his sand wedge like a bat, Rodgers took the mighty cut of a ballplayer foul-tipping a high outside pitch. The ball simply dropped to a lower limb. So he swung again and ticked it for strike two. The ball dropped down to the next branch below. It took him two more "foul tips" before the ball dislodged and fell to the ground.

"It kind of went down a series of floors like an elevator, five to four, four to three, three to two, until it reached the ground," said Rodgers. "As it was working its way down, you could hear the elevator bell ring. Actually, the bell was going off in my head. I got it on the ground in five, on the green in six, and two-putted for an eight." He finished the round with a disappointing 74.

Nevertheless, Rodgers came charging back and actually took the lead in the final round, only to lose by two strokes—the difference between his not taking a penalty drop and his attempting to blast out of the tree.

Asked if he ever fretted over his decision, Rodgers replied, "You just can't let those things kill you."

Willie Chisholm

1919 U.S. Open

In one of the most rock-headed decisions in golfing history, Willie Chisholm chose to play a nearly unplayable lie—and wound up setting a U.S. Open record in futility.

Even though his ball was lodged against a rock, the Scottish pro was determined to play it out rather than take a drop for a one-stroke penalty.

41

As a result, he shot an atrocious 18 on one unforgettable hole—the worst score ever recorded for a par-3 in Open championship history.

Chisholm's disaster came on the 185-yard par-3 eighth hole at Brae Burn Country Club in West Newton, Massachusetts. Between the tee and the green was a deep ravine with a bubbling brook that snaked its way through large rocks. Despite this ominous hazard, most Open golfers managed to par the hole. In fact, several birdied it.

Chisholm's playing partner, Jim Barnes, belted a nifty drive to the green and then stepped aside to watch the Scot tee up. Unfortunately, Chisholm took a little too much turf. His ball carried the brook by two or three feet and then fell on the steep bank below the green, coming to rest against a boulder.

After reaching his ball and surveying the situation carefully, Chisholm made two decisions he'd live to regret—he'd play it out and aim for the green. He called for his trusty niblick, the nine-iron. Meanwhile, Barnes took up a position in the middle of a wooden bridge that spanned the ravine, where he could look down at Chisholm and help him count his strokes.

After a few practice swings, Chisholm took his stance, held a firm grip on the club, and swung. Unfortunately, the clubhead crashed into the boulder, giving off a few sparks and a sharp ring, and bounced over the ball. The impact sent shock waves jangling through his body. This should have been warning enough that perhaps this wasn't the best approach. But the hard-headed Scot tried the same shot again—with the same bone-jarring results.

Now, beyond all reason, Chisholm, acting like a man possessed, began hacking away at the boulder. With each frustrating swing of metal striking rock, the niblick's club head gained a new dent, and like Chisholm's face, became red-hot. Sparks darted and rock chips flew, but the ball didn't budge. Barnes, who didn't know whether to laugh at Chisholm or feel sorry for him, marveled that the niblick's hickory shaft hadn't broken.

It took a weary Chisholm 13 strokes before he came to the conclusion that he could reach triple digits on this hole alone if he kept this up. So he changed tactics. Instead of trying to play toward the green and blast through the rock, he chose to chip the ball away from the boulder. To his everlasting relief, he hit the green on his 15th stroke. Then he staggered to the green, exhausted and perspiring so much he looked like he had been golfing in the brook.

But at least there was relief on his face, having finally made it to the green. With a totally unwarranted trace of optimism, Chisholm hoped to end this unmitigated disaster with one putt. But he three-putted.

Now came the real test. Chisholm tried his best to count up all his strokes, but since he had been working in the bottom of the ravine for the greater part of thirty minutes, he was not sure exactly how many he had taken. So he asked Barnes for the score.

"Willie, you took 18 for the hole," said Barnes.

Chisholm stared at him in disbelief and said, "Oh, Jim, that can't be so. You must have counted the echoes."

Harry Bradshaw

1949 British Open

Harry Bradshaw might have won the 1949 British Open if only he had decided to stay away from the bottle. Don't get the wrong impression. He didn't drink from the bottle; he hit it.

But his thinking couldn't have been any worse had he taken a nip or two before the first tee.

In the second round of the championship at Royal St. George's in Sandwich, England, the chubby Irishman was just one off the pace when he came to the 451-yard par-4 fifth hole. Unfortunately, he cut his drive slightly into the right rough. It was no big deal. Or so he thought.

When Bradshaw found his ball, he couldn't believe his eyes. The ball had bounced into a broken beer bottle! The bottle was standing upright with the neck and shoulder broken off and jagged edges sticking up.

He didn't quite know how to handle this extraordinary dilemma. However, he made one quick decision—he opted not to ask for a ruling from the officials, because it just wasn't his nature to do so. He came from the old school. Since he'd got into this trouble himself, he'd get out of it himself. The idea of seeking help from the rule book simply offended him.

After fifteen minutes of studying the situation, Bradshaw chose to play the bottle and ball. He boldly reached for his blaster, closed his eyes to protect them from flying glass, and swung with all his might. The bottle splintered into dangerous shards that flew in all directions. But the ball moved only 25 yards.

The bottle wasn't the only thing that had shattered. So had Bradshaw's nerves. Shaken by this unlucky incident, he missed the green with his next shot and took a double-bogey six. He later confessed that it took him six more holes before he recovered his composure, finishing with a shaky 77 for the round. He regained his fine golfing form in the final two rounds and wound up in a playoff, which he then lost to South African Bobby Locke.

Had Bradshaw not been so bull-headed and sought a ruling, he could have treated the bottle as an obstruction and moved it. Under the existing Royal and Ancient code, he could have placed the ball on the ground where the bottle had been, without penalty.

But Bradshaw chose to hit the bottle. He admitted that his predicament and the emotional effect it had on him for the rest of the second round cost him the championship. But even long after he retired, Bradshaw still refused to admit that he had made the wrong choice by not seeking a ruling.

"If I had sent for a ruling," he said, "I might have won the championship. But it wouldn't have been right."

Billy Joe Patton

1954 Masters Tournament

Billy Joe Patton would have become the first amateur ever to win the Masters—if only he had decided to play it safe. But Billy Joe chose to outbrazen the field and prove to the crowd that he was no lily-livered, weak-kneed coward.

But in the end it was his own bravado that betrayed him.

The brawny, bespectacled North Carolinian captured the gallery's heart with his powerful swing, affable grin, and constant chatter. He kept

AP/WIDE WORLD PHOTOS

up a running dialogue with spectators, telling them before each shot what he was "a gonna do."

To everyone's surprise, Billy Joe led after the second round. After slipping in the next round, he charged into the lead on the final day at Augusta National with a blistering 32 on the front nine, including a hole in one at the sixth.

The crowd began shouting, "Billy Joe, you're gonna win it! You're gonna win it!" Amazingly, he had passed two of the greats at the turn, Ben Hogan and Sam Snead. Leading at the 13th, Patton learned that Hogan had just made a double-bogey six on the 11th. Now if Billy Joe could just play prudently, his name would be etched in golfing history.

For his second shot on the devilish par-5 13th, Patton had a nasty, side-hill lie. Conventional wisdom called for a lay-up shot. He studied the shot momentarily while the crowd shouted at him to be cautious. Then, whipping a four-wood out of his bag, he told the gallery, "I didn't get where I am playin' safe."

"He's goin' for the green!" shouted a spectator. Murmurs of concern spread throughout the crowd and turned to groans when his bold but misguided shot plopped into Rae's Creek.

Still as brash as ever, Billy Joe removed his shoes and socks, rolled up his trousers, grabbed a wedge, and marched into the water (see photo). He got set twice to hit the ball, but then he came to his senses and realized it was too risky. He took a one-stroke penalty and, still barefoot, pitched up to the green, where he two-putted for a calamitous bogey six.

However, he birdied the next hole. Victory was well within his grasp when he studied his second shot on the par-5 15th water hole. "I may go for it, and I may not," he drawled. "It all depends on what I elect to do on my backswing." Despite cries from fans to play it safe, Patton again chose to court danger—and splashed his shot into the pond in front of the green. He two-putted for a bogey six.

Billy Joe parred in from there, but his day was gone, never to come again at the Masters. He finished at 290—one behind Snead and Hogan. Had he chosen to go for par on the 13th and 15th, he would have achieved an historic two-stroke victory. (Snead won the playoff with Hogan, 70–71).

Looking back, Patton said, "I wouldn't play it any differently. I was elated to play as well as I did. I'm almost delighted I lost, in fact. Otherwise," added Patton, who treasured his amateur status, "I might have turned pro."

CRUEL RULES

Although it measures only six inches by three inches and weighs a shade over two ounces, The Rules of Golf *has the power to kill the fortunes of pro golfers. The little rule book has cost many a Tour pro a top title or big money. For "The Most Inglorious Infractions Ever Committed,"* The Golf Hall of SHAME *inducts the following:*

Tom Watson
1980 Tournament of Champions

Tom Watson committed a careless rules violation during the 1980 Tournament of Champions. It didn't seem like a big deal. But what made the offense so embarrassing to him was that it occurred just months after publication of a book he wrote on, of all things, the rules of golf!

As Watson and Lee Trevino walked off the 12th tee in the final round, a considerate Watson told his playing partner, "Lee, you're playing the ball too far forward in your stance." Trevino, whose game that day was faltering, thanked him for the advice.

A few holes later Trevino conducted a brief interview with Bob Goalby of NBC, which was televising the tournament. While on the air, Trevino mentioned that Watson had given him a helpful tip on the 12th hole. Neither Trevino nor Goalby mentioned that this was a clear violation of the rules.

However, a viewer at home well versed in the rules knew that giving advice to or asking advice from a competitor is a breach of Rule 9–1a. The viewer immediately called LaCosta Country Club in Carlsbad, California, to alert officials to the violation. Word didn't reach tournament director Jack Tuthill until minutes after Watson had won the prestigious event. Just as Watson was about to sign his scorecard for a 71 in the

AP/WIDE WORLD PHOTOS

scoring tent, Tuthill asked Watson if he had given advice to Trevino. Watson confessed he had and was penalized two strokes.

The penalty merely cut Watson's winning margin from five strokes to three. But the violation left him with egg on his face because, he admitted, he should have known better. After all, he coauthored the book *The Rules of Golf Explained and Illustrated.* In his book, which was published a few months before the tournament, he said he learned his lesson about that particular rule at the 1968 U.S. Amateur Championship.

"Although I was only 17, I had played enough golf by then to know better," Watson wrote. "I was paired with Mike Taylor, from Mississippi. We hit it off well and began to help each other by telling what clubs we used. On one hole, I yelled clear across a fairway to Mike to ask him what he'd hit and Mike answered. USGA official Pete Tufts could hardly believe his ears. Mike and I were each penalized two strokes—I for asking for advice, and Mike for giving it."

Watson added, "There's no surer nor more painful way to learn a rule than to be penalized once for breaking it."

Only in Watson's case, it was twice.

Lou Graham

1970 Westchester Classic

In one stomach-churning moment, Lou Graham fell victim to such an astounding series of mishaps, he could have used a lawyer. Graham broke four rules in just ten seconds and was socked with six penalty strokes.

In the second round of the 1970 Westchester Classic at the Westchester Country Club in Harrison, New York, Graham hooked his second shot on the 12th hole. His ball landed about 30 yards short of the green on the side of a steep bank where it came to rest up against a TV cable.

Delicately, Graham lifted the cable, moved it farther up the bank, and then studied the green for his chip shot. Suddenly, someone in the gallery shouted, "Look out! Look out!" Graham, fearing that an errant shot was about to hit him, ducked. Then he turned around and saw what the spectator was really yelling about—Graham's ball was rolling down the bank.

Dismay turned to horror for Graham as he helplessly watched the ball hit his bag. It had been placed there by his caddie, who was standing farther down at the bottom of the bank. After bouncing off the bag, the ball continued on its merry way, and when it reached the bottom, Graham's caddie instinctively picked it up. Then he tossed it back to Graham who reached out and caught it.

"I'm thinking to myself, 'Lou, what happened?' " recalled Graham. "God almighty, I was standing there with the ball in my hand, thinking, 'What did I just do?' "

Graham knew he had done something wrong, but wasn't quite sure what. First, he asked his playing partners, but they didn't have the

UPI/BETTMANN NEWSPHOTOS

foggiest idea. So he summoned PGA Tour official George Walsh to make a ruling.

Spectators started yelling at Walsh, "Lou didn't do anything wrong!" and "Don't penalize him!" Walsh turned to the crowd and snapped, "Just hold it down!" Then he listened to Graham's woeful account of his ball's misadventures. "Okay," Walsh told the golfer, "that's two strokes for the ball rolling without having it marked, and two more for the ball hitting the bag. The caddie picked it up so that's another two strokes, and you caught the ball, so add another two shots. That totals up to eight."

"What?" sputtered Graham incredulously. "That can't be!"

"No," said Walsh, correcting himself. "You would have had to pick up the ball yourself anyway, so it's only six shots."

"Oh, c'mon, George," pleaded Graham. "I didn't touch it. It just started rolling."

"Well, I'm not sure," confessed Walsh. "Tell you what. It may only be four. Then again, it may be six. I'll get back in touch with you before you finish your round. Play it as a six-shot penalty for now."

With only seven holes left to play, a shell-shocked Graham knew he had to rack up a few birdies to overcome the penalty strokes in order to make the cut. He made only one more birdie.

"When I got back to the scorer's tent, I couldn't find George," Graham recalled. "This was back before they used walkie-talkies on the course. Fifteen minutes went by and I was asking everyone if they had seen George. I was holding up my playing partners because they had to attest to my card before leaving the scorer's tent. So finally I just signed with an added six strokes on the 12th and left the tent."

Those penalty strokes were fatal because he missed the cut by only one shot. Graham was in the locker room clearing out his belongings when Walsh rushed in and said, "Hey, Lou, you didn't sign your scorecard yet, did you?"

"Of course I did. I waited as long as I could."

"Gee, that's too bad. We figured it out, and you only had a four-shot penalty."

Graham would have made the cut after all. But it was too late now to change his scorecard. Recalled Graham, "I can laugh about it now. Heck, I've told that tale so many times that it was almost worth missing the cut."

Tommy Bolt

1959 Memphis Invitational Open

Tommy Bolt was once fined for farting.

Bolt's indiscretion occurred during the 1959 Memphis Invitational Open at Colonial Country Club. Standing on the green with his playing partners, Bolt was waiting for them to putt first. With customary considerateness, the gallery's voices fell to a hush. Suddenly Bolt lived up to his nickname of Thunder and let one rip. He didn't just discreetly and silently break wind; he unleashed a reverberating howler.

The spectators burst out laughing. But not everyone was amused. "That's disgusting," said one of the golfers. Apparently, several people in the gallery felt the same way. In fact, they were so offended they reported Bolt to the tournament officials.

When word reached fellow golfer Bob Rosburg, who was then chairman of the players committee, he felt compelled to act. Although there was no rule directly forbidding farting, Rosburg decided that Bolt—the 1958 U.S. Open champion—nevertheless could be fined for conduct unbecoming a professional golfer.

With some reluctance, Rosburg caught up with Bolt and said, "Tom, you and I are good friends, but we've had this report that you farted on the green."

"Oh, yeah," said Bolt. "I just had to do it."

"Tom, you can't do that, not while a man is playing. You got turned in. I have to fine you."

Bolt shook his head and bellowed, "Damn it! You guys are trying to take all the color out of the game!"

Rosburg, who recalled the story at a roast for Bolt in 1988, said he fined Tom $250, "which was a big fine in those days."

When asked to comment about the incident, all Bolt would say was, "That story got blown out of proportion."

George Burns and Harpo Marx
Hillcrest Country Club, Beverly Hills

Irrepressible funnymen George Burns and Harpo Marx caused an uproar over a rules violation at the swank Hillcrest Country Club that is still talked about today.

One sweltering summer day, as George and Harpo headed for the first tee, they decided to doff their shirts, unaware that this was against club rules. Quicker than a drive down the fairway, an offended club member known for his snobbery complained to the caddie master.

He, in turn, rushed into the clubhouse to report this grievous breach of club etiquette to the haughty Greens Committee. Shocked that golfers on the course would dare expose their hirsute bosoms, the committee scampered out to the course and caught up with the bare-chested pair on the second tee.

Waving the sacred Hillcrest book of regulations under the noses of the twosome, the snooty committee chairman announced to George and

Harpo, "You can't play like that. It clearly states in our book of regulations that shirts must be worn by members at all times."

"But we can appear on a public beach without tops," George protested. "Why must we wear them here?"

"Sorry," said the chairman. "No shirts, no play."

Reluctantly, George and Harpo donned their shirts before the smug Greens Committee—having dealt with the day's most serious offense—returned triumphantly to the clubhouse.

Meanwhile, back on the course, the two comedians decided that a little civil disobedience was in order.

Five minutes later the caddie master burst into the clubhouse with news even more disturbing than before. "Come quick!" he shouted to the Greens Committee. "Now those actors are out there playing without pants!"

Once again the committee charged back onto the course and found, to their horror, Harpo and George blithely walking along the fourth fairway wearing only their shirts and undershorts. But no pants.

"Just what in tarnation do you think you're doing?" thundered the chairman. "You can't play golf here without wearing any pants!"

Harpo snatched the venerable book of regulations from him, thumbed through it, and then innocently asked, "Where in here does it say members must wear pants?"

After much stammering and grumbling, the committee realized it was stumped, and revised the regulations on the spot. Ever since then, male members have been allowed to play without shirts. However, players must wear pants on the course at all times.

Paul Farmer

1960 Texas Open

Paul Farmer "puttered" into trouble so deep he couldn't climb out.

The thirty-two-year-old California touring pro was rolling along in the 1960 Texas Open, shooting three rounds of par or better at San Antonio's Fort Sam Houston course. He fired a two-under-par 70 in the third round, but it didn't last long. When he came off the course, officials gave him the crushing news that he had to tack on another 18 penalty strokes to his score.

All because he had changed putters at the turn.

As he walked off the ninth green, Farmer was irritated by paint flaking off the brass heel of his putter. "This is bugging me," he told his playing partner, Dave Marr. "I'm going to change putters."

"I don't think you can change putters unless you accidentally break it," said Marr.

"Well, I think I'm within my rights," Farmer countered. "The flaking has made my club unfit for use, and under the rules, a club can be replaced for that reason." So he did.

Farmer couldn't have been happier when he finished the day only one stroke behind the leader. He had visions of winning, or at least finishing high in the money and collecting a decent paycheck. But his daydream was suddenly shattered by PGA tournament director Harvey Raynor, who ruled that mere flaking didn't render the putter unfit.

As a result, Raynor charged Farmer two strokes per hole for the last nine—18 in all—that the new putter was used. The ruling inflated Farmer's 54-hole total of 213 into a sad 231, which knocked him completely out of the running.

The incident so unnerved Farmer that he forgot his nine-iron the next day in the final round. Realizing there was little he could do to salvage his horrendous score, Farmer at least salvaged his sense of humor.

Spotting Raynor on the course, he asked, "Say, Harvey. Do I get back two strokes for every hole I play without my nine-iron?"

Rules Were Made to Be Broken

Payne Stewart: When he was trying to qualify for the Tour in 1980, he hit the wrong ball in two tourneys. "Both times I was in the rough, I saw a Titleist, and hit it," he said. "It cost me two strokes each time. Then I invested 69 cents in a Magic Marker, and haven't done it since."

Fuzzy Zoeller: At the 1981 Memorial, Zoeller was walking through an enormous hazard in which his ball had landed. He was still about 100 yards away from his ball when he came to a stream. Struck with what he thought was a simple but smart idea, he picked up a rock to put in the stream so he could step across it without getting wet. Instead, he got nailed with a two-stroke penalty for picking up loose impediments in a hazard. Fuzzy admitted his brain was just that. "I was in the ozone," he said.

Ben Crenshaw: In the first round of the 1986 U.S. Open, Crenshaw's second shot lodged in a bush, so he declared it unplayable and dropped it. Then, he admits, "I blanked out." His ball hit the ground and began to roll. Under the rules, the ball has to be redropped if it rolls more than two club-lengths. Crenshaw was sure it would roll that far but didn't wait to find out. He stopped it and picked it up. "I wish I hadn't seen that," said an official. Ben was penalized two costly strokes and finished tied for sixth instead of fifth.

Tony Jacklin: Jacklin was penalized for his good intentions at the 1974 British Open. He was among the leaders when his ball rolled into a rabbit scrape, so he took a free relief and dropped the ball two club-lengths. The ball rolled down a slope into a much more favorable lie. Conditioned not to seek undue advantage from the rules, he picked up his ball and dropped again. Only then did he learn that his first drop had put the ball in play. He was hit with a two-stroke penalty and was so rattled he dropped out of contention.

Bob Dickson: On the second hole of the second round of the 1965 National Amateur, Dickson noticed that he had an extra club in his bag, one over the legal limit of fourteen. He immediately told officials, who promptly penalized him four strokes, two strokes for each of the first two holes. The penalty was devastating—Dickson went on to lose the championship by one stroke. It was especially hard to take because the extra club was not Dickson's at all. Someone had mistakenly placed it in his bag.

Betty Bush: Bush hooked a drive that lodged high in a tree during the 1953 Women's Open. So she summoned a young man from the gallery, who fetched a ladder, climbed up the tree, and retrieved the ball. He threw the ball down to Bush, who then proceeded to hit it back onto the fairway. But officials were not amused and penalized her two strokes for playing it from where the good samaritan threw it down.

Jack Fleck: Fleck was breezing along with the leaders at the 1960 Western Open when he hooked his shot into a water hazard. He took several practice swings at a piece of paper before it dawned on him that he was in a hazard. Fleck was penalized two strokes per practice swing for a total of eight, giving him a whopping 13 strokes on the hole. From then on he wasn't a factor in the tourney.

Sam Snead: At the 1959 Buick Open, Snead tapped in a one-inch putt with one hand—while he unthinkingly held the pin with the other. He was assessed a two-stroke penalty for hitting an attended flag stick. It cost him a fourth-place finish.

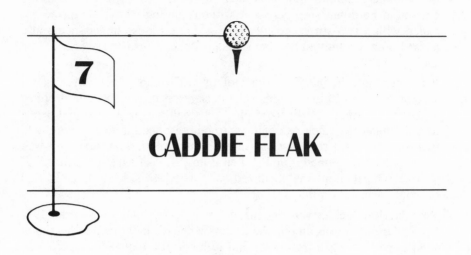

CADDIE FLAK

Time after time the fortunes of pro golfers have fallen not by any bad shot, but by the bumbling of their caddies. Sometimes bag-toters pose a greater hazard than the deepest bunker. For "The Silliest Screw-ups by Caddies," The Golf Hall of SHAME inducts the following:

Rod Munday's Caddie

1939 Thomasville Open

If this had been a baseball game, Rod Munday's caddie would have been hailed a clutch hitter. But this was golf, and he was cursed as a big-time bumbler.

Munday, a hard-luck club pro from the Country Club of York, Pennsylvania, was trying to win some desperately needed cash in the 1939 Thomasville Open at the Glen Arven Country Club in Georgia. Holding his own among the leaders, he was at even par when he reached the par-4 18th hole in the third round.

After hitting a perfect drive, Munday socked a four-wood that carried to the back of the green. The ball hit the face of the sloping green and bounced into a sand trap. When he reached the bunker, Munday noticed that his ball was pin high and very close to the cup. However, the trap was so deep that he could not see the surface of the green. But he could see the flag.

"Hold the flag," Munday instructed his caddie. "And then pull it out once you see the ball in the air. Make sure you don't let the ball hit the flag stick, understand?"

"Yes, sir, I sure do," replied the caddie, a young lanky lad with only a season or two of experience under his belt.

Munday walked into the sand trap and settled into his stance. "Yank that pin out fast," he shouted to his caddie, "because I'm going to sink this blast shot. And remember, don't let the ball hit the stick."

Munday played his best cut shot with nearly a full swing. It looked perfect, flying softly straight toward the flag. In fact, he thought it might drop in for a birdie. But just as the spectators were about to applaud this marvelous shot, they gasped at a sight so incredible they knew they would never see another like it in their lifetimes.

When the ball landed and bounced five feet short of the hole, the caddie obediently jerked out the pin. But as he quickly turned to move away, he swung the flag stick parallel to the ground like a baseball player taking a mighty cut. Unbelievably, the caddie accidentally whacked the ball dead center with the pin on the first bounce and knocked it about 40 yards into the woods!

Munday stood speechless, trying to comprehend what he had just witnessed. When it finally sunk in, Munday was crushed. But being the gentleman that he was, he said nothing audible to his caddie—although under his breath Munday cursed him. Then the golfer trudged off into the woods, made a remarkable chip shot, and two-putted for an eight, which included a two-shot penalty for the "base hit."

Although Munday handled the stunning mishap with extraordinary aplomb, he never fully recovered from the shock. In the final round he played poorly and finished out of the money in a tie for 29th place.

Jack Nicklaus

1983 U.S. Open Qualifying Round

Jack Nicklaus is one of the game's greatest golfers, but as a caddie he leaves something to be desired. And his sons will be the first to admit it.

The Golden Bear was caddying for his fourteen-year-old son Gary (shown together in photo on next page) at Hunter's Run in Boynton Beach, Florida, during a qualifying round for the 1983 U.S. Open. At the first tee Nicklaus, as any good caddie should, checked the clubs in his son's bag to make sure it held no more than the legal limit of fourteen. "When I count, I never count each club," Nicklaus said later. "I just look for the numbers on the clubs. I didn't see anything in Gary's bag that didn't belong there."

But he did spot something on the third hole. While his son was mulling over which club to use on the next shot, Nicklaus asked, "What do you think, Gary?"

Gary replied, "A four-iron."

Nicklaus agreed. He reached into the bag and winced at what he saw. "Which one would you like to play? Yours or mine?" Somehow, Nicklaus's MacGregor Muirfield "Limited Edition" four-iron had wound up in Gary's bag along with the youth's own four-iron. That meant he had 15 clubs—one too many. Under medal play, that infraction costs two strokes per hole, with a maximum of four. In this case, Gary was assessed four penalty strokes.

"We had played the night before and I had looked through his bag, but I just missed it," Nicklaus recalled. "It was my fault. Here I've preached to my kids all these years to do everything right; not to make stupid mistakes. So what do I do? I make it for him. Gary didn't think it was funny at the time, but it is funny that I'd make such a silly mistake."

As it turned out, Gary's total of 155 would not have qualified him, even without the penalty.

Nicklaus hasn't had much luck as a caddie to his sons. In 1982's U.S. Open qualifier he was caddying for another son, Jack Jr.—and lost his son's ball on the very first hole.

St. Andrews Caddies

1946 British Open

The caddies at the venerable Royal and Ancient Club of St. Andrews have nursed a reputation as the world's best, able to read the grass right down to the roots. But at the 1946 British Open, Sam Snead went through the R & A's caddies like a bucket of range balls. He had to fire them because they deliberately tried to sabotage his game.

They were miffed over an offhand remark made by the country-bred West Virginian—known at the time as "golf's most famous hillbilly." He made his innocent remark during his first trip to Scotland. While heading to the Open on a train from London with fellow golfer Lawson Little, Snead spotted a run-down, weedy fairway in the midst of some gray, craggy moors. He tapped the knee of a proper well-dressed English gentleman who was sitting across the aisle and said, "Say, that looks like an old, abandoned golf course. What did they call it?"

The blood drained from the Englishman's face. "My good sir!" he replied haughtily. "*That* is the Royal and Ancient Club of St. Andrews, founded in 1754! And it is not now, nor ever will be, abandoned!"

"Holy smoke, I'm sorry," said Snead sheepishly. He turned to Little and whispered, "Down home we wouldn't plant cow beets on land like that."

Snead had just maligned the most famous links in the world. Worse yet, he had made his insulting remark to a very proud duke who was not about to let this matter rest.

"The British papers made a fuss about my remark, and from then on I was dodging reporters who had the knife out for me," Snead recalled. "The only place over there that's holier than St. Andrews is Westminster Abbey." *The London Times* jabbed him with this stinging line: "Snead, a rural American type, undoubtedly would think the Leaning Tower of Pisa a structure about to totter and crash at his feet."

Then the St. Andrews caddies joined in the act and made life miserable for Snead during the first few days of the Open. While other golfers raved about how great the caddies were, Snead went through five caddies in four days because, he declared, "mine were a bunch of bums."

The first caddie tried to annoy Snead by whistling between his teeth whenever the golfer putted. The bag-lugger further vexed Snead by wiping the ball clean with the same rag he used to blow his nose.

So Snead traded him in for Scotty, supposedly the finest caddie at St. Andrews. But he did his best to screw up Snead's game. During the qualifying round, they came to the tee of a par-3. There were no yardage markers back then. "It's a five-iron, it is," the caddie told Snead.

"That can't be a five-iron," said Snead, looking at the short distance to the green. But he knew that disagreeing with a Scottish caddie would result in a scene. Such a caddie was known to angrily throw down the bag if the golfer didn't agree on the club selection. Nevertheless, Snead took an eight-iron—and still hit his shot ten yards behind the hole.

On the next hole, a par-5, Snead was going for the green on his second shot when Scotty said, "A three-iron, it is." So Snead cranked a three-iron about 220 yards, but it fell 20 yards short of the green. "Hey, Sammy!" shouted a voice from the gallery. "Scotty's trying to bungle [trick] you!"

Once again Snead demanded that the caddie master find him a new bag-toter. The golfer was given a caddie who had been found sleeping in a bunker. He was useless. He failed to make the starting time because he got drunk the night before and wound up in jail. Snead's fourth caddie lasted a round before he was fired for demanding more money.

The fifth caddie stuck with Snead for the rest of the tournament—only after Snead bribed him by promising to pay him 200 pounds. (First-place money was only 600 pounds.) Snead told him to keep his nose clean and gave him one other order: "If I should ever ask you what club to use, look the other way and don't answer."

Despite all his caddie troubles, Snead won the Open by four strokes. When Snead walked off the green with the victory, his caddie told him, "I'd like to have the ball. I've never caddied for a champion in my life." After Snead graciously handed him the ball, the caddie beamed with joy and gushed, "I'll treasure it for the rest of my life."

The next morning Snead learned that his caddie had sold the treasured ball for 50 pounds.

Dale Douglass's Caddie

1981 Kemper Open

Because his caddie got lost, Dale Douglass was forced to tee off with his putter.

Consequently, Douglass, a three-time winner on the PGA Tour, owns the unofficial record for the longest putt in tournament history—150 yards.

Shortly before he was slated to tee off in the first round of the 1981 Kemper Open at Congressional Country Club in Bethesda, Maryland, Douglass was hitting balls on the practice range. "When I was finished practicing," Douglass recalled, "I took my putter and told my caddie, who was a local, 'I'll see you on the first tee.'

"For the tournament, the nines were reversed from the way the membership had been playing them. I went ahead to the first tee, and he took my clubs and went to what he *thought* was the first tee but was really the 10th tee. The tees are only 200 yards apart, but there's a steep hill between them."

Douglass waited and waited. No caddie. Finally, when his name was called, the golfer had no choice but to tee off or face disqualification. "All I had with me were my putter and some golf balls," he said. "I had used that same putter since 1965, and I was worried I might break it. It was a Tommy Armour. I was concerned about the shaft because it was old and kind of rusty and not built to hit a drive.

"But I hit my drive real straight. It just didn't carry the rough, otherwise it might have rolled 180 yards."

Meanwhile, his caddie was frantically trying to find Douglass. When the bag-toter finally figured out he blundered, he hightailed it over to the first tee. But by then it was too late.

Douglass, scanning the gallery for any sign of his caddie, walked as slowly as he could toward his ball. He didn't relish the thought of hitting a fairway shot with his putter. Just then the red-faced caddie caught up with him.

"The caddie was embarrassed," recalled Douglass, who ended up bogeying the hole. "There wasn't much I could say. It was funny then, and it's still funny."

Peter Mack

Winged Foot Golf Club, Mamaroneck, N.Y., 1934–45

No caddie was more irritating, more annoying, more exasperating than Peter Mack. That's because it was his job to deliberately aggravate humorless, hotheaded, or mean-spirited golfers who were in need of an attitude adjustment.

Golfers fed up with a no-fun playing partner hired Mack for $50 to caddie for the sourpuss. Usually, by the time the victimized golfer had completed the front nine, he was so infuriated by Mack's incompetence that he wanted to club him.

That was never more apparent than the day in 1938 when Mack drove a golfer nuts during a round at Winged Foot Golf Club. Mack was "assigned" to an intolerable member known only as Mr. Brown, a quick-tempered golfer whom his playing partners said "would start fighting if you as much as breathed while he putted."

When Mack arrived at the first tee, Brown was appalled at the sight of his caddie. Looking like he'd spent a week of solitary confinement in the caddie shack, a grungy, unshaven Mack was dressed in a filthy pair of trousers. Vaseline was oozing through the sleeves of his dirty, long-sleeved undershirt.

Brown, looking with disdain at his new caddie, asked, "What's that on your arms?"

"Oh, nothing," said Mack. "Just a bad case of eczema."

Brown immediately strode over to the caddie master and demanded a new caddie. But the caddie master, who knew all about Mack, said he was sorry but there were no others.

Miffed that he was saddled with such a scuzzy-looking caddie, Brown stalked to the first tee. He snatched his driver from Mack's hand and discovered the grip was all greasy. "What's this?" he asked. Mack, who had secretly covered Brown's grips with Vaseline earlier in the locker room, feigned ignorance. "Gee, I don't know. It must be something inside the bag." So he turned the bag upside down, dumping out all the clubs and balls. Then Mack slowly picked everything up and cleaned the grips as a foursome played through.

By now Brown was smoldering. He angrily grabbed his driver from Mack—and then sliced his first shot into the woods on the right. Just to vex Brown, Mack began looking in the rough on the *left* side of the fairway. The incensed golfer screamed at him to search the woods on the other side. Once again another foursome was waved on.

After finding the ball, Mack gave Brown an iron and then stood almost on top of him. Brown, now flushed with anger, snarled through clenched teeth, "Stand back!" He then proceeded to miss the ball completely.

"Mr. Brown," said Mack innocently. "Willie Turnesa [1938 U. S. Amateur champion] played here yesterday and had a 67. He never looked up once like you did on that shot."

Brown blew a fuse and unleashed a torrent of expletives before his playing partners calmed him down. It took the foursome an incredible thirty minutes to play the first hole.

On the second tee, Mack was washing Brown's ball when it became stuck in the ball washer. So the caddie whipped out a screwdriver that he just happened to bring along and took apart the ball washer. Of course, they had to let another foursome go through.

Brown's temperament soared from ire to rage at the fourth tee when he discovered that his driver had been left behind on the third tee. Brown seethed as he waited for Mack, who slowly sauntered back to retrieve the club.

Brown was seeing so much red, he could barely see the ball, and his game fell completely apart. On the sixth green, he missed an easy three-foot putt, whereupon Mack threw the bag down in the bunker and said indignantly, "I won't caddie for a guy who can't make a short putt like that!" But after some pleading by Brown's playing partners, Mack agreed to continue his bag-toting.

Not until the foursome reached the hole farthest from the clubhouse did Mack pull his best stunt. Without anyone noticing, he poured peroxide on his lips and began foaming at the mouth. As Brown was lining up a putt, Mack let out an unearthly yell and toppled backwards into a sand trap, where he feigned unconsciousness. No matter how badly Brown wanted to leave Mack there—in fact, he would've liked to have buried him there—Brown helped lug the caddie's limp body all the way back to the clubhouse in sweltering 90-degree heat.

Weary and spent of all emotion, Brown plopped down on a clubhouse barstool and turned to drink to wipe out the memory of the previous few hours. While nursing his third cocktail, Brown looked up and couldn't believe his eyes. There at the bar was Mack, healthy, clean-shaven, and clad in a knit shirt and pressed pants. Only then did Brown realize that he had been the latest victim of the "Clown of the Caddies." With no anger left in his spleen, Brown meekly shook his head.

Mack, a professional actor who died in 1952, was paid $50 for his "caddying." When one of Brown's playing partners asked Mack where his next job was, Mack replied, "Tomorrow I go to Montauk Point and teach some snooty guys how to fish. I'll make sure the lines get all mixed up and that some of these fellas get hooks in their wrists and everything. Fishing is tougher than caddying. I charge $100 for that."

Striking Caddies

1914 Tournament for the Bamberger Trophy

The caddies at the New Siwanoy Golf Club in East Chester, N.Y., were a real riot—literally.

At the 1914 Tournament for the Bamberger Trophy, a hundred caddies went on strike, and when their demands weren't met, they stormed the course and disrupted play. They beat up strike-breaking caddies, swiped golf clubs out of bags, stole golf balls off greens, and hurled disgusting epithets at the players. In fact, the caddie riot turned so ugly that the golfers had to finish the tourney under police protection.

Trouble began brewing when the hundred golfers in the tournament called to their favorite caddies to take the bags and start out. "But before we go," each boy said to his prospective employer, "I want to tell you that we have raised our rates. It's no longer fifty cents a round. From now on we work for seventy-five cents a round." In each case, the demand for the increased rate was refused and another caddie was called. The second caddie also insisted on the higher rate.

"Well then," an angry club official announced to the caddies, "you're all fired!"

"The hell we are," retorted one of the leaders of the caddies. "We're on strike!"

Apparently forewarned that the caddies might strike, the club had earlier found dozens of eager young boys willing to tote bags for fifty cents. They were immediately put to work—and put in danger.

Meanwhile, the strikers stomped off and then quietly regrouped near the fourth hole. Armed with old brassies and niblicks and sticks and stones, the caddies lay in wait to ambush the scabs and golfers alike. Then, like golfdom's version of Little Big Horn, the strikers charged out from the rough, the woods, and the bunkers onto the fairway, attacking the young strike-breaking caddies first.

"The boys were pummeled with such enthusiasm that they quickly withdrew, dropping clubs and bags," said a *New York Herald* account. Streaming across fairways and greens, one squad of strikers scooped up every ball that was hit while another squad pillaged golf bags.

"The players were called vile names, and some of the women became so frightened that they ran to the clubhouse for protection," said the *Herald*. "When a fat player came puffing along toward the fifth hole and tried to hit a ball with his brassie, which was the only stick he had left, one of the strikers shouted, 'Don't let the guy get the ball!' In a jiffy, half a dozen caddies were after the ball, and it was soon out of sight."

Finally, frantic club officials called the police, who wielded night sticks to drive the strikers from the course. Once calm returned and reason prevailed, the tournament continued, but under police protection. As for the strikers, all except the ringleaders reluctantly went back to work—at the old pay rate of fifty cents.

Caddie Shock

Shortcut to Trouble

Raymond Floyd's caddie took a shortcut to save energy and a few minutes. As a result, Floyd lost his temper and two strokes.

During the first round of the 1987 Tournament Players Championship, the caddie took a shortcut from the 10th green to the 11th fairway. He then placed the bag on the edge of the righthand rough. Ray, meanwhile, went to the 11th tee with only his driver.

As luck would have it, Floyd whacked his drive about 260 yards—smack dab into his own golf bag! The 1989 Ryder Cup captain was penalized two strokes for striking his own equipment. He chewed out his caddie and eventually fired him.

Way Out of Line

In the 1954 British Amateur at Muirfield, American Frank Stranahan infuriated the caddies because he refused to take their advice. In fact, he fired a bag-toter after each round for arguing with him over club selections.

The next caddie he hired got even with him at a hole where the green was hidden by a high ridge. Stranahan sent his caddie to the top of the ridge to line him up in the direction of the green. When the caddie reached the spot, he waved and Stranahan hit directly over him. Thinking he made a fine shot, the golfer was shocked when he reached the ridge—the caddie had lined Stranahan up to a thick patch of ferns.

The caddie then dropped the golf bag at Stranahan's feet and headed for the caddie shack, saying, "Now, sir, if you think you know so much about golf, let's see you get yourself out of there."

Finders Weepers

The caddie for British golfer Maurice Bembridge wanted him to win so badly that he ruined the golfer's chances at the 1968 PGA Championship.

In the first round, Bembridge, a Ryder Cup player for the British team, had sliced a drive into the rough. After a lengthy search, his caddie announced that he had found the ball, so Bembridge played it. But a few minutes later someone in the gallery found Bembridge's real ball.

Upon questioning, the caddie tearfully confessed that he had deliberately dropped a new ball in the rough. Bembridge sacked him on the spot and reported the matter to officials.

Ironically, because of Bembridge's honesty, the officials had no choice but to disqualify him.

Ask and He Shall Deceive

Sam Snead was playing the par-5 16th hole at Firestone Country Club in Akron, Ohio, on a windy day when his second shot fell far short of the lake in front of the green.

"How far to the green?" he asked his caddie.

"Well," the caddie answered, "yesterday I caddied for Jay Herbert in a practice round and he hit an eight-iron."

Snead grunted, pulled out the eight-iron, and swung. The ball plopped right in the middle of the lake.

Snead was furious. "You mean to tell me that Jay Herbert hit an eight-iron from here?" he testily asked his caddie.

"Yes, sir, he sure did," came the reply.

"Where'd his shot land?" Snead demanded.

"Oh," said the caddie quite innocently, "Mr. Herbert hit his ball in the lake, too."

Never Mind the Ball,
Where Are My Clubs?

While playing a round of golf on the Queen's Course at Gleneagles, Scotland, USGA official George Smith and his wife arrived at the 13th hole. The hole calls for a blind tee shot across a ravine.

Mrs. Smith sent her drive off to the right into a well-nurtured stand of heather. Her caddie dutifully hacked his way into the thick heather and searched for the ball. After several minutes passed, Mrs. Smith declared the ball lost and decided to play another. As she headed back toward the tee, she noticed that her caddie was still searching determinedly through the heather. "You can stop looking for the ball now," she told him.

"It's not the ball I'm looking fer, mum," he replied. "It's yer clubs I've lost."

What We Have Here
Is a Failure to Communicate

On the first day of the 1965 Pensacola Open, Bob Goalby's regular caddie was sick, so the golfer was assigned a local bag-toter who apparently had never caddied before.

With the ground wet from an overnight rain, Goalby was digging up divots as big as sirloin strips. After a few holes Goalby ordered his caddie, "Make sure you pick up those divots, son."

On the back nine the caddie was lagging farther and farther behind and struggling with Goalby's bag. I know the bag's not that heavy," the golfer told him.

"But it keeps getting heavier," complained the caddie.

"Let me see that bag," said Goalby with rising irritation. Sure enough, it was heavy. Then he discovered why. The caddie had taken Goalby's orders to pick up the divots too literally. Each divot was carefully stuffed inside the zippered pockets of Goalby's bag.

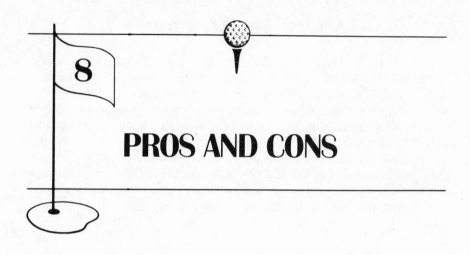

PROS AND CONS

Golf courses are often nothing more than open-air green casinos where bets are made as often as ten-inch putts. More hustling takes place on the fairway than at a singles bar. For "The Trickiest Bets Ever Made on the Golf Course," The Golf Hall of SHAME *inducts the following:*

John "Mysterious" Montague
Lakeside Country Club, North Hollywood, 1937

In the zaniest one-hole match ever played, Bing Crosby lost to John "Mysterious" Montague—whose only clubs were a rake, a shovel, and a baseball bat.

The world's most famous crooner was singing the blues when he lost a wacky bet to the mysterious one. A jolly 300-pound hustler who played golf with Hollywood's biggest stars, Montague was the Lakeside club champion in 1934–35. He was nicknamed "Mysterious" because he never talked about his past, had no visible means of support, and hated to be photographed. Once when he was in position to break the course record at Lakeside, he picked up on the 18th hole rather than risk any publicity over setting the record.

Ironically, Montague's greatest notoriety came in a private bet he made with Crosby. He had just beaten Bing, who himself was a five-time club champion and a scratch player. The two were sitting at the bar at Lakeside when Der Bingle moaned to Montague, "You don't give me enough strokes."

"Forget the strokes," said Montague. "I can handle you with a rake, a shovel, and a bat."

This appealed to Crosby, if for no other reason than it was such an outlandish proposal. After agreeing on a bet of $5 a hole, Bing grabbed his golf clubs while Montague hauled his unorthodox golfing equipment to the par-4 tenth hole.

Holding a baseball bat in one hand, Montague tossed his golf ball into the air and walloped it an amazing 350 yards. Unfortunately, it rolled into a sand bunker directly in front of the green.

Bing whacked a so-so drive straight down the fairway about 210 yards. Then, with his seven-iron, he put his ball only 15 feet from the cup. Montague strode into the bunker with his shovel and in one smooth motion scooped the ball up onto the green about six feet from the hole.

Bing putted first, but his birdie attempt slipped three feet past the cup. Then Montague walked up to Bing's ball and knocked it away, saying, "That's a gimme." Next, he took his rake, turned it so the prongs pointed up, and pushed his ball in for a birdie three.

A stunned Bing shook his head and quit on the spot. "That's it. I've seen enough," he grumbled.

It was this incredible game that unmasked Mysterious Montague. After his great rake-shovel-and-bat triumph, his photograph appeared in the eastern press. The New Jersey police recognized him as Laverne Moore, wanted in connection with a 1930 roadhouse holdup. Montague was arrested and extradited. But a delegation of Hollywood pals, including Crosby, came to his defense. They said his clean record in California proved that he had been rehabilitated. The judge agreed and released him.

Bing continued to play golf with Montague—on the condition that Mysterious play only with regulation clubs.

Titanic Thompson

It's a sure bet that no golfer was a more conniving, scheming hustler than Titanic Thompson. From the 1920s until he died in 1974, Titanic swindled big spenders, club pros, and even notorious gangsters out of their fat bankrolls.

While the top touring pros of his day were making $30,000 a year, Titanic often picked up $50,000 in a few weeks because he was a superb golfer and an even better con man. Usually he'd beat his pigeon right-handed by a stroke or two and then innocently double the stakes with an offer to play left-handed—which happened to be his best side.

Titanic didn't make bets, he offered "propositions"—ones that were almost always fixed. Take his long-putt scam, for instance, which netted him tens of thousands of dollars. Titanic would bet that he could make at least three out of five putts from 30 feet away. He usually holed four out of five. What his victim didn't know was that on the previous night, after the green had just been watered, Titanic had placed a heavy water hose from the edge of the green to the cup and kept it there until early the next morning. This created a nearly imperceptible trough. Titanic simply sent those balls right through the trough and into the hole.

Once, Titanic made a bet with two New York gamblers that he could hit a golf ball an unbelievable 500 yards. He had to drive it off a tee but the ball did not have to land in the fairway. So Titanic picked a very special tee at a Long Island course on a hill overlooking a lake. Since it was the dead of winter, the lake was conveniently frozen. Titanic whipped out his driver and drove the ball onto the icy lake. It was still rolling when he pocketed the money.

One of his best-known hustles occurred in Tulsa in 1932 when he was challenged by a big, powerful club pro who insisted on a handicap. "Instead of strokes," Titanic told the pro, "I'll let you drive three times off each tee, and then you can play the best drive." The pro gladly accepted, and the match began—with a bet of $1,000 a hole.

Playing the best of his three drives, the pro won the first seven holes. But then his game fell apart and Titanic swept the last 11 holes and picked up $4,000. "A big hitter has about twenty swings in his system," Titanic confided to his cronies later. "After that, his game is just a prayer and a stagger. If the big guy hadn't been so greedy, he could have figured that out for himself."

In one of his favorite ruses, Titanic showed up at a Florida country club looking pale and wan. He "accidentally" let it slip that he had been sick and hadn't touched a golf club in months. Nevertheless, he accepted a high stakes challenge with some of the club members. On the course he blew them away. "Those fellows thought that because I wasn't sun-burned, I hadn't played," Titanic later explained. "I didn't bother telling them I'd been practicing like crazy, wearing a big hat, long sleeves, and gloves on both hands."

One day in 1935, Titanic hoodwinked a wealthy rancher out of $10,000 in a game. Thompson and the rancher came up to the 18th hole all even and both golfers laid up short of the green on their second shots. However, the rancher's ball landed in a sand trap. Before the rancher reached the trap, Thompson whipped out a ten-dollar bill, gave it to his caddie, and said, "Run up there and drop this in the trap." Moments later, after the rancher entered the trap, he reappeared waving the ten-dollar bill and shouting, "Look what I found in the trap!" Titanic shook his head sadly and cited an official rule that was in force back then that said a golfer could not remove anything from a sand trap, not even a rake, until after his shot. "Gee, I'm sorry," he told the rancher, "but that'll cost you a stroke. You lie three." Titanic won the match by virtue of that one penalty stroke.

The six-foot, 160-pound hustler—whose real name was Alvin Thomas—neither drank nor smoked, and refused to have his photo taken even with friends. Although the name of Titanic Thompson was known in every clubhouse from New York to California, his face was familiar only to a handful of cronies—and victims.

Titanic often relied on accomplices. Once, in the middle of a casual clubhouse conversation, he mentioned that he had seen a golfer in a wheelchair who could outplay any club member. After hearing the inevitable scoffs, Titanic bet a sizable bundle that the cripple could beat the naysayer. The next day Titanic produced his "cripple," an unknown young pro who was not handicapped and had secretly practiced in a wheelchair for weeks. Titanic won the bet and split the take with the fake cripple.

Titanic handpicked his "caddies"—who were really talented young golfers a year or two away from turning pro. He dressed them in bib overalls and sent them ahead to clubs known to have high-rolling gamblers on the links. By the time Titanic arrived, his caddies knew how well everybody in the club could play. So he made his bets and won $5,000 Nassaus.

But he wasn't finished with his victims. "Hell," Titanic would tease a golfer whom he'd just beaten, "even my caddie can beat you." In most cases the insult triggered a new series of wagers. Then his "caddie" would beat the pants off the poor mark and split the winnings with Titanic. Many of his caddies went on to make names for themselves on the PGA Tour, such as Lee Elder, Dutch Harrison, Horton Smith, and Ky Laffoon.

Even off the course Titanic duped golfers. Paul Runyan, winner of the PGA Championship in 1934 and 1938, recalled seeing Titanic in action at a clubhouse in Hot Springs, Arkansas. "Titanic was just sitting there, eating walnuts and having an idle conversation with the gambling characters that always seemed to flock around him," said Runyan. "He got down to his last walnut and was just about to crack it open when he offered to make a bet that he could throw it over the clubhouse. Well, he had all the action he could handle. Of course he won the bet. That last walnut just happened to be filled with lead."

Payne Stewart

1988 Leukemia Classic

Payne Stewart had the pants beat off him after making a wacky wager during an exhibition match.

Stewart, winner of the 1989 PGA Championship, played LPGA members Cindy Figg-Currier, Deborah McHaffie, and Chris Johnson in the 1988 Leukemia Classic, a six-hole charity event at the Hercules Country Club in Wilmington, Delaware.

Before teeing off, Stewart suggested to the women that he take the

70

three of them on. "I'll play [against] your best ball," he said. "What would you ladies like to bet?"

Figg-Currier, staring at Stewart's trademark pastel plus fours, said, "Why don't we play for your knickers?"

"That's fine," he replied. "My knickers against your shorts. Whoever loses takes them off on the 18th green and gives them to the winner."

Stewart immediately went one up when he holed out with his sand wedge for an eagle on the first hole. The girls came back with a birdie on the second hole to even the match. After the next hole was halved, the girls birdied the fourth hole to go one up. The fifth was halved, leaving Stewart one down as the foursome reached the final green. He needed to win the hole to keep from losing his pants, but McHaffie made a birdie putt to clinch the match.

Stewart winced and then said, "Well, a bet is a bet." So in the middle of the green he unbuckled his knickers. Then, to the squeals of the gallery, he dropped his pants. Now down to his white Jockey underwear, he stepped out of his beige plus fours and handed them over to the winners. In celebration, Figg-Currier put on Stewart's knickers and the two posed for photos. Then Stewart, pulling his shirttail down over his shorts, scampered back to the clubhouse.

DELAWARE CHAPTER, LEUKEMIA SOCIETY OF AMERICA

"I made the bet and I had to pay off," recalled Stewart. "I'm glad my shirttail was long. I had to walk kind of huffily back to the locker room."

Recalled Figg-Currier, "It was worth the wait for him to take off his knickers."

Added John Riley, cochairman of the event sponsored by the Delaware Chapter of the Leukemia Society of America, "The women in the gallery told me that Stewart looked almost as good as [former Baltimore Orioles pitcher and Jockey model] Jim Palmer."

Although Stewart lost, everyone was a winner. After he and the women autographed his knickers, they were auctioned off at the charity event for a cool $1,500.

Chi Chi Rodriguez

Chi Chi Rodriguez could hustle the feathers off a bird; and do it in such a clever way that the hustled pigeon would walk away smiling.

Fortunately for the thousands of easy marks on the golf course, Chi Chi has chosen to make his living playing tournament golf. But he's not above making a friendly wager now and then that relies on P. T. Barnum's philosophy, "There's a sucker born every minute." At least with Chi Chi's bets, all the loser can do is laugh at how cleverly he was duped.

"Sometimes it's fun to win a friendly little wager, especially with guys who pinch nickels so hard the Indian rides the buffalo," said Chi Chi, who recalled two of his favorite "can't-lose" bets.

Once, in 1966 at the Dorado Beach Country Club in Puerto Rico, he closed out his playing partner, a New Yorker named Ross, on a $2 Nassau on the 17th hole. At the 18th tee, Chi Chi made Ross a proposition:

"I'll give you a chance to get even. I'll bet the whole Nassau on this last hole. I'll give you two strokes if you give me one throw."

Ross, a three-handicapper, readily agreed. They both hit the green on the par-4 18th with their second shots. Ross was 15 feet from the hole; Chi Chi was 20 feet away.

Ross, smiling confidently, said, "Okay, take your throw now, Cheech."

"I plan to do just that," replied Chi Chi. He calmly walked over to Ross's ball, picked it up, and threw it into the ocean. "Okay, you lie three down there."

A few years later at the Doral Country Club in Miami, Chi Chi was conducting a golf clinic when one of his students, a big Irishman named Jerry, challenged him to a long-distance driving contest. "You can't outdrive me," Jerry boasted.

The five-foot-seven-inch, 135-pound Puerto Rican sized up the big galoot and figured Jerry would be an easy fish to reel in. "I'll let you hit a drive and a wedge shot," said Chi Chi, "and I'll bet that you still won't be able to catch up to my drive."

Jerry took the bait, believing the bet would be impossible to lose. Hitting first, he swung so hard that he popped the ball up.

Chi Chi, slyly reeling in the big fish, said, "I'll even let you hit again."

This time Jerry's ball exploded off the tee and soared 320 yards. There was no way, thought Jerry, that Chi Chi could come close to matching that drive; and even if by some fluke he could, Jerry still had another shot.

Chi Chi teed up his ball, gazed at Jerry's ball in the distance, and shook his head. Then he turned around 180 degrees—and whacked his ball in the opposite direction. Said a grinning Chi Chi, "Now let's see you catch up to that!"

Tenison Park

East Dallas, Texas

Tenison Park reigned for years as the hustle capital of the world.

The municipal course in East Dallas became a casino on the green where hustlers had names like Fat Man, Ace, Big Mickey, and the Fly; where touring pros were "shipped home C.O.D."; where a former caddie named Lee Trevino won bets by using a Dr Pepper bottle off the tee; and where legendary gamblers kept hours as regular as bank vice-presidents.

From the 1920s through the 1960s, Tenison Park was known in select circles as a free port of open action. "They used to play for $100 a nine, $10 a hole with presses," recalled Erwin Hardwick, former longtime pro at Tenison Park. "That was when a man was working his tail off to earn $35 a week."

It was here that hustlers hustled hustlers. Each one had his own gimmick.

For theatrics, the Redeemer soared to the top of the leader board. Dressed in black and thumping a Bible, the bearded "preacher" appeared one day from behind a pecan tree on the 12th hole and confronted a foursome of hustlers with shouts of, "Repent! Lay aside the sticks of the devil!"

After a few minutes of heated debate, the Redeemer, who swore he had never touched a "devil's stick," reluctantly agreed to play them—for money. He punctuated his golf with shouts of "Hallelujah!" and "Lord, put the right club in your servant's hand!" Early in the match, when one of the golfers hit a fat one, the Redeemer hit one a little fatter just to build up the pot. When it was over, he lightened their troubled souls and wallets of hundreds of dollars of "filthy lucre."

Fat Man, a short, squat jelly roll of a golfer, deliberately looked like a slob so opponents would underestimate his skill on the links. One of his tricks was to mix up his headcovers, putting the two-wood cover on a four-wood. That way, when he hit a four-wood, his opponent would think it was the two-wood. The opponent would then hit a two and send the ball flying over the green.

The best hustler at Tenison was Dick Martin, said veteran Tenison golfer Don Millender. "He was the kingpin of Tenison. He worked at golf his whole life." Somebody once asked Martin why he didn't turn pro, and he replied, "Because I can't afford it."

To hustlers such as Martin, golf was a job not unlike the actuary business. They calculated the odds, studied the risks, and invested no more than they could afford.

Martin's secret was handicapping. Once, to entice some high-handicap players, Martin let them play their second shots from where his tee shot landed. Naturally, Martin could outhit any one of them, but on this

UPI/BETTMANN NEWSPHOTOS

particular day he "unexpectedly" developed a terrible hook. Most of his tee shots hooked into the woods, except a couple that barely dribbled off the tee. There was no way his challengers could recover. Martin won the nine-hole match in five straight holes.

Even Tenison Park caddies learned to hustle. Dizzy Dean, the great St. Louis Cardinals pitcher, became an easy mark. Dean always requested one particular caddie, even though it was well known among the Tenison insiders that the caddie always bet against Dizzy. But this failed to shake Dean's confidence until, one day in a tight situation, the caddie handed Dean a two-iron where a five-iron was all that was needed. Dean lost the match.

Besides being fleeced by fellow golfing gamblers, getting robbed was also an occupational hazard for hustlers. One day, Fat Man was down $600 to the Fly when a gunman emerged from the woods near the third hole. "Your money or your life!" snarled the thug. Fat Man quickly whipped out his wad of money, peeled off six $100 bills, and handed them to the Fly. "There, now we're even," said Fat Man before both were relieved of all their cash.

The decline of heavy betting at Tenison Park began after Nassau Nick was led off the course in handcuffs in 1953. He was an ex-FBI man using his old identification card to cash checks to finance his growing golf-hustling empire.

Up until then the side action was getting out of hand. "It got so bad that [nonplaying] bettors were using cars to follow the players around the course," recalled Hardwick, the Tenison pro. "I put a stop to that, and I started charging green fees for anyone who wanted to watch. What really made it bad was the kids from Woodrow Wilson [a nearby high school] took to coming over and following the action. They'd hear all that big talk, and they'd think: 'Why go to school if money is that easy?' It was bad for golf."

The most famous Dallas schoolboy-turned-caddie-turned-hustler-turned-pro is Lee Trevino. In his early days as an assistant pro, in 1964, he began playing with a taped-up family-sized Dr Pepper bottle (see photo). "I could hit the ball 90 or 120 yards and could keep it high or low," he recalled. "It was great on a par-3. I used to bet members that I could beat them scratch using this taped-up bottle, hitting the long shots fungo style and putting pool style. I was deadly. I won some money on that. But I didn't hustle anyone. They all knew what I could do with that bottle, and they took their chances.

"But contrary to popular belief, I've never been a big gambler. But I'll tell you one thing. The biggest bet you'll ever make in your life is for the last dollar in your pocket—and I've made that bet more than a few times."

Hope Jest

Comedian Bob Hope pulled off one of the cleverest scams in golf history.

He was playing with his friend, producer Sam Goldwyn, at Lakeside Country Club when Goldwyn blew an easy two-foot putt. In a rage, Sam hurled his putter into a bush, vowing never to use that club again. As Goldwyn stormed on to the next tee, Hope quietly picked up the discarded putter and slipped it into his own bag.

When it was Hope's turn to putt on the next green, he used Goldwyn's putter and sank a 20-footer. Sam was impressed and asked if he could try Hope's putter. Hope obliged. After examining the club carefully, Goldwyn tried a few practice putts and then said, "I like this putter very much. Will you sell it to me?"

"Sure," said Hope with a perfectly straight face. So Goldwyn happily—but unwittingly—bought back his own putter for $50.

In the Pocket

In 1977, two years before golfer Jim Thorpe joined the PGA Tour full-time, he played in a big money game with amateur Brian Stavley at East Potomac Park in Maryland.

"There were several guys who bet the money—about $5,000," recalled Thorpe, the Tour's fourth-leading money winner in 1985. "I was playing for the black guys, and Brian, a young white kid, was playing for the whites. They [the bettors] were all over the course watching us. We were dead even going into the eighth hole, when Brian hit his drive into the rough. We looked and looked but we couldn't find his ball.

"While we were searching for the ball, a buddy of mine [who was one of the bettors] came over to me and whispered, 'He'll never find his ball.' I said, 'What do you mean?' And he said, 'I've got his ball in my pocket.'

"Brian had to go back to the tee and hit another ball. He made bogey. Back then we'd do anything to win."

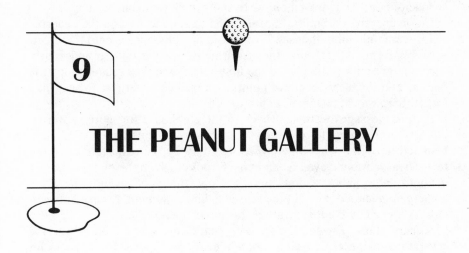

THE PEANUT GALLERY

The way some tournament spectators behave, the gallery ropes ought to be used for hanging. Golf fans have displayed some of the weirdest, wildest, rowdiest behavior this side of a Motley Crue heavy-metal concert. For "The Wackiest Behavior by a Tournament Crowd," The Golf Hall of SHAME *inducts the following:*

MacDonald Smith Fans
1925 British Open

MacDonald Smith was defeated by his own fans!

In the last round of the 1925 British Open, more than 15,000 boisterous fans swarmed over the course to cheer him on—yet they unwittingly did everything they could to stop him from winning.

Smith was considered the best golfer who never won a major tournament. Time and again he came excruciatingly close to capturing a big title only to come up a stroke or two short. But now a coveted British Open victory was well within his grasp. At the start of the final round he was leading his closest competitor, Long Jim Barnes, by a fat five strokes. No one else even had a chance. Teeing off well ahead of Smith, Barnes finished with an indifferent 74. All Smith had to shoot was a 78 and the big title he had sought for so many years would be his.

It seemed all of Scotland had closed shop and assembled at Prestwick, the historic links on the country's west coast, to root Smith to victory. Although the Scottish-born Smith had emigrated to the United States years earlier, the Scots still considered him their own. And they descended upon Prestwick en masse to show their enthusiastic support.

Unfortunately for Smith, he was timed to start just when the Glasgow trains were unloading thousands of golf-loving passengers onto the Prestwick platform. All at once they swarmed onto the course and nearly surrounded Smith as he played the first hole. Then they rushed along the fairway and fought for vantage points. Yet in their eagerness to see, they forgot there was MacDonald Smith to consider.

Frantic messages were sent back to the clubhouse for more stewards, but few were keen to volunteer. Smith was so bustled, jostled, and hemmed in by the whooping crowd that only by the exhortations of the few stewards was he even given enough room to swing. Not once did the uncontrollable gallery allow him the opportunity of seeing where his longer shots landed, nor did the fans give him a moment's peace between strokes so he could concentrate on his next shot.

So many fans crowded the fairways that Smith was forced to wait for several minutes between each shot while stewards cleared a path for him to play through. Cheering spectators continued to spill into bunkers and onto the greens. They bumped him, talked to him, and slapped him on the back between shots. And as the day wore on, these bits of well-intentioned encouragement only reminded Smith that the tournament was slipping away from him. Distracted, unable to concentrate, and robbed of his rhythm, Mac Smith shot an 82.

He never came close to winning a major tournament again.

The lesson wasn't lost on tournament officials. In 1926 they began to charge a gate fee to keep the crowd to a manageable number. But the change came much too late for MacDonald Smith.

The Ditz

1940 Hershey Open

There's always someone in the crowd whose course is short a few flag sticks. One such ditzy fan cost Byron Nelson a second-place finish at the 1940 Hershey (Pennsylvania) Open.

Nelson was locked in a tie for second when he teed up at the 17th hole, a par-5 dogleg to the left lined by trees. Rather than hit down the fairway and shoot for par, Lord Byron decided to gamble by taking a shortcut. Gunning for a birdie, he lofted a towering drive that cleared the trees on the left.

The gallery at the tee oohed and aahed at this beauty of a drive which seemed certain to land on the fairway in perfect position for his approach shot. Nelson couldn't help but beam proudly as he acknowledged the applause.

When he walked around the bend of the dogleg, he expected to easily spot his ball. But to his dismay, he saw the ball marshals searching in the rough. Then he, his caddie, and other stewards went hunting, too, but to no avail. Members of the gallery hadn't seen where the ball had landed because they were either at the tee when he hit it or were heading for a vantage point at the 17th green. After several long, frustrating minutes, the search was called off.

Puzzled by the fate of his ball, Nelson trudged back to the tee and hit his second shot. Once again he drove over the trees, smacking an almost identical drive as before. Only this time the ball landed on the left side of the fairway near the rough—exactly where Nelson thought his first ball had come to a rest. Despite losing a stroke, Lord Byron still managed to par the hole. But that was little consolation because that lost ball cost him a birdie and he wound up finishing third, one stroke behind the second-place finisher.

It wasn't until a few weeks later that the mystery of the lost ball was solved. Nelson was relaxing at home reading his fan mail when a check fluttered out of an envelope he had just opened. To his surprise, the check was for $350.

The accompanying letter was from a man who had attended the Hershey Open with his girlfriend. He said it was his girlfriend's first tournament, and although she didn't know much about golf, she sure enjoyed it, especially the souvenir she found.

It seems they were walking through the trees that line the 17th hole when, without his noticing it, she spotted a golf ball near the edge of the fairway and picked it up as a memento. "Mr. Nelson," said the letter writer, "that was the very same ball that cost you second place. For that reason, please accept my check for $350, the difference between second and third place."

Gene Sarazen Fans

1923 PGA Championship

Gene Sarazen won the 1923 PGA Championship thanks to the blatant cheating of his too-loyal fans.

Sarazen, one of America's greatest golfers, was not aware of this partisan chicanery. But he was certainly aware that the gallery at the Pelham (New York) Country Club desperately wanted him to win. After all, he had grown up in the area, where people knew him under his given name of Eugene Saraceni. They all considered him their local hero.

For this 36-hole match-play event, Sarazen, the defending champion, was pitted against his keenest rival, Walter Hagen, the 1921 winner. Unfortunately for the Haig, he had to contend not only with his gifted opponent, but also with Sarazen's fans, including several of the club's red-sweatered caddies who were loyal to a fault—literally.

The first sign that the fans would do anything to help their man win came on the 14th green, which was guarded by a water hazard. Sarazen hit his second shot much too strong. The ball was headed toward the pond when a quick-thinking fan in a red sweater stuck out his foot and stopped the ball from rolling into the water.

"I should have had an easy win [on the 14th hole], but I managed to halve the hole," Hagen said in his autobiography. "After that, I kept my eyes open for boys in red sweaters." But he couldn't keep watch over all of them.

Hagen and Sarazen were tied after 36 holes and went to a sudden-death playoff. They halved the 37th and came to the 38th, which was bordered by houses on the left. The gallery uttered a collective moan when Sarazen hooked his drive over a fence. The last he or Hagen heard of the ball, it was rattling in between the houses. Officials declared it out of bounds, so Sarazen hit another shot, this time right down the fairway. Recalled Hagen, "With the two-stroke penalty he had incurred by his out-of-bounds shot, I figured I could win easily if I played safely down to the right."

Confident that Sarazen could never recover from the penalty, Hagen hit a safe drive to the middle of the fairway and walked jauntily toward his ball. But to his shock, Hagen heard people in the gallery shout that Sarazen's first ball had been found—and, even more incredibly, it rested inside the fence!

When Hagen walked over to take a look, he was flabbergasted. Sarazen's ball was lying neatly on top of the grass a few yards from where kids had made a huge hole in the fence to sneak through onto the golf course. "Witnesses" said the ball had indeed gone out of bounds but it "miraculously" had bounced back through the hole in the fence.

Sarazen had no way of knowing that the ball had been conveniently moved by an "outside agency"—one of his devoted but misguided fans who had tossed it back in play. All Sarazen knew was that by a twist of fate he had been given a reprieve. He didn't have to take a penalty shot after all.

Buoyed by this tremendous break, Sarazen hit a magnificent second shot within a foot of the hole for a certain birdie three. Hagen shook his head in disbelief. Then, obviously shaken by this stunning turn of events, the Haig put his second shot in a trap, short of the green. "Suddenly, an easy victory for me had turned into defeat," he recalled. "There was nothing for me to do except to walk over and congratulate Gene."

And what of Sarazen's out-of-bounds ball that so amazingly bounced back into play? Said the Haig:

"I've never to this day doubted that such luck could happen, but having Gene's ball jump back through the fence and be found teed up could have resulted only from the hand of the good Lord or one of the red-sweatered caddies roaming the course.''

The Cherry Hills Bandit

1960 U.S. Open

A sneaky little thief emerged from the gallery to swipe a valued club from under the nose of Tommy Bolt during the 1960 U.S. Open.

The bandit—a scrawny but sly kid about ten years old—had slipped past the gate and onto the Cherry Hills course in Denver not so much to watch the golfers, but to filch one of their clubs. Time and again he eased ever so close to a golf bag only to be shooed away by a caddie or a marshal.

Sitting behind the fairway ropes on the 12th hole, the kid was wondering how he'd ever snatch a club when suddenly Tommy Bolt's shot splashed into a pond. Bolt, who wasn't nicknamed ''Thunder'' for his sweet disposition, soon erupted in a heated argument with a USGA official over exactly where he should drop his ball for the penalty shot.

The kid was struck with a brainstorm. He knew that once Bolt began stewing, it was only a matter of time before the terrible-tempered golfer would reach the boiling point and fling one of his clubs in a fit of rage. If and when that happened, the club would be easy pickings.

The kid watched with growing anticipation as Bolt three-putted the hole and proceeded to bogey the next hole. With every stroke, Bolt's anger mounted. Twice it looked like he would lose it, but Bolt somehow maintained his composure.

By the 18th hole the kid had all but given up, when, to his delight, he watched Bolt hook not one but two drives into the lake. This could be it, the boy thought. Bolt, his eyes ablaze with fury, stalked from the tee to the edge of the lake and peered at the watery grave of the two lost balls. Then, still clutching his driver, Bolt reared back and hurled the club into the water.

Seizing the moment, the kid took careful note of the exact location where the club hit the water and he belly-flopped into the lake. He dove to the bottom and thirty seconds later triumphantly resurfaced with the driver. The gallery, which had given Bolt a few jeers and boos because of his temper, now cheered as the boy worked his way to the bank.

Bolt, feeling somewhat sheepish over throwing a fit—and his club— managed a slight smile as he walked toward the dripping wet boy. ''Thanks, son, I sure appreciate you fetching my driver,'' Bolt said. ''It's my favorite one.''

Without saying a word, the kid took a few quick steps to his left. But when Bolt turned toward him, the boy darted to his right and scooted around the surprised golfer. Then, with the driver still in his hand, the boy lit out across the fairway as the gallery roared with laughter. A spectator gave the kid a leg up over the fence, and that was the last anyone ever saw of the Cherry Hills bandit—or of Bolt's favorite driver.

Sam Snead Fans

1938 Westchester Open

In the only golf tournament Sam Snead ever won that he wished he'd lost, souvenir-hungry fans accosted and mauled him before he escaped with his life by diving over a hedge.

"I was right in the middle of the first golf riot I'd seen," recalled Snead. "I was at the mercy of a mob."

The attack happened at one of the weirdest tournaments ever founded—a 108-hole marathon called the Westchester Open at Fenway Country Club in New York.

About 2,000 fans had paid admission to watch the six-round tourney. But the gallery swelled to an additional 10,000 people too cheap to pay but eager to watch. In the final round they charged through the gates, collapsed the fences, and stampeded onto the course to overwhelm police, marshals, and golfers.

"You couldn't swing a club without almost beheading somebody," recalled Snead, who was hanging on to a one-stroke lead over Billy Burke as they played the finishing hole. Wielding cane poles, the police did their best to hold the raucous gallery back. But Snead's approach shot triggered a 100-yard dash by fans in the front line trying to be the first to reach the green. Unfortunately for Snead, the ball bounced off one of the running spectators and landed in a muddy depression 40 yards from the green.

"How the hell can I hit out of here?" Snead asked a policeman. But the cop didn't answer. He was too busy fighting a losing battle with the gallery. The seething mob then smashed the cane poles and ran the cops off the course. Despite the surging crowd, Snead swung his eight-iron in a short arc with a choked-down grip and, considering the circumstances, made a brilliant shot onto the green.

Snead managed to par the hole for an unheard-of total of 430 (remember, this was for 108 holes) and beat Burke by two strokes to claim the $5,000 first prize. But within seconds, Snead was regretting that he had won.

Before he could reach the safety of the clubhouse, he was engulfed in a sea of swarming fans who spilled out onto the green. Snead could see they were not appreciative golf fans. They were obnoxious members of an ugly, unruly mob dead set on snaring a souvenir of Slammin' Sammy. One wild group had rushed the green to fight for his ball.

Recalled Snead, "Hundreds of people were piled up and the cries were awful. 'Get off, you're breaking my leg!' you'd hear someone yell. 'Oh, my God, my back!' Then there'd be a cracking noise. It was like fourteen football teams scrimmaging. I don't know how many they hauled away in ambulances.

"They grabbed me, and the next thing I knew they had me on their shoulders and a man was yelling, 'The winnah!' Then I was on top of people and being hauled this way and that until I thought my spine would break."

His shouts of protest went unheeded. Like starving wolves attacking a lamb, fans tried to rip his shirt and tear off his shoes. Fearing for his life and unable to get down from their shoulders, Snead frantically looked for a way out. Suddenly he spotted a high hedge behind the green that looked like it would provide safety on the other side. So he stood up on someone's shoulders and made a desperate leap over the crowd and over the hedge.

What he didn't know—but quickly found out—was that beyond the hedge was a 15-foot drop off to a lower tee. Snead sailed through the air, crash-landed, and cartwheeled to the tee below. More scared than hurt, Snead picked himself up and scampered 75 yards to the clubhouse. He didn't stop running until he was safely behind locked doors. "I had never seen anything like it," he recalled. "The gallery went absolutely berserk!"

The Pickpocket

1936 U.S. Open

In the boldest crime ever perpetrated during a major golf tournament, a sticky-fingered spectator picked the pocket of player Les Madison as he walked down the fairway!

But there's a bizarre twist. Although Madison lost an undisclosed amount of money, the real victim was actually playing partner Lighthorse Harry Cooper. "The gallery and [the theft] cost me the Open," declared Cooper.

Cooper was burning up the Baltusrol course in the final round of the 1936 U.S. Open. Playing at a record-setting pace, he looked like a sure winner. Even playing partner Johnny Bulla thought so. On the 15th hole, Bulla told Cooper, "Harry, all you've got to do to win is be standing up when you finish. You can't lose. It makes no difference what you do from here on in." But it made a big difference what a slow-moving spectator and a sneaky fingersmith did.

"The gallery started coming from all over when they heard I was winning, but there were no gallery ropes and nobody was there to handle the crowd," Cooper recalled. "People were standing in the pathway and wouldn't get out of the way on the short 16th. I said to hell with it and hit." The ball was heading straight for the pin when it struck a spectator who made a halfhearted attempt to get out of the way. The ball bounced off him into a sand trap. Instead of an easy par, Cooper had to settle for a bogey four.

Shaking off the bad break, Cooper parred the next hole. Then on the par-4 18th, he put his second shot onto the green. A par would give him a 283 and break the then U.S. Open record of 286. Cooper, whose biggest win up to then had been the 1932 Canadian Open, felt the adrenaline surge through his body. He couldn't wait to hole out. So, surrounded by spectators, he marched briskly toward the green.

Meanwhile, playing partner Les Madison, who also had hit his second shot onto the green, was walking with the crowd huddled around him when he felt his back pocket. "My wallet!" he shouted. "Where's my wallet?" He started to retrace his steps, thinking maybe it had fallen out, but in his heart he knew it had been swiped. He begged spectators for help in finding the pilferer, but no one had seen a thing.

Back on the green an anxious Cooper was cooling his heels. "I had to stand there for eight solid minutes before I could putt, waiting for Les," he said. "Of course, I was nervous and wanted to go. I stood there for a long while, and apparently it affected me because I three-putted from 35 feet. I wasn't mad at Les. It wasn't his fault."

Nevertheless, Cooper shot 284, a record that lasted for all of 30 minutes. While Cooper was receiving premature congratulations in the clubhouse, Tony Manero finished with a blistering 67 to snatch the victory away from him.

It was the first time in U.S. Open history when two playing partners felt robbed.

The Panicky Spectator

1952 Palm Beach Round Robin

Cary Middlecoff lost a tournament after a bizarre turn of events that would have been even more hilarious to him if it hadn't been so costly.

In one of those freak shots, his ball landed inside the pocket of a spectator who, in a panic, took off running, and then, not knowing what else to do, threw the ball into the rough.

It all happened during the 1952 Palm Beach Round Robin at Wykagyl Country Club in New Rochelle, New York, where 16 pros played 36 holes in medal match play.

In the final round, Middlecoff was leading when he reached the 223-yard par-3 16th hole. He took out his trusty two-iron and aimed for the flag. But the ball faded to the right, bounced off the fringe of the green,

and landed right in the jacket pocket of a middle-aged spectator who was sitting on the ground.

At first the man didn't seem to know what had happened. But other members of the gallery began laughing and pointing at him. As the crowd moved in for a closer look, his eyes grew wide and, thinking that he had somehow done something wrong, the frightened man bolted from the gallery.

Quickly, other spectators ran after him, shouting, "Stop!" "Get back here with that ball!" and "Put the ball down!" The last command seemed to do the trick. Without missing a beat, the fleeing man pulled the ball out of his pocket and threw it away. Then he kept right on running.

Meanwhile, back at the tee, Middlecoff couldn't figure out what all the fuss was about. When he finally reached the green, he looked around and then asked, "Where's my ball?"

"Some spectator ran off with it," said a galleryite.

"What?" asked Middlecoff incredulously. "Where'd he go?" The crowd pointed to a hill behind the green. Middlecoff trekked up the hill and found his ball in a rocky lie right beside a tree about 20 yards from where the ball had hit the spectator.

Recalled Middlecoff, "I got a very bad ruling. They made me play it from where it lay. I should have been able to drop it from the spot where it hit the guy near the green. So I made a double-bogey five and lost the hole.

"Things like that happened all the time back then, before gallery ropes. It didn't make you happy at the moment, but there wasn't much you could do about it.

"I believe I would have won. Instead, I finished second and lost about $1,000 in prize money. Back then, that was some decent money. If that had happened today, can you imagine how much money that'd cost you?"

Gallery of Horrors

1934 U.S. Open: On the 12th hole, Wiffy Cox's drive landed on a coat that a spectator had thoughtlessly left on the fairway. When the fan saw the ball resting on his coat, he ran onto the fairway in embarrassment and whisked away the offending garment. Unfortunately, he also whisked away Wiffy's ball, which then rolled into the rough.

1937 Masters: In the final round, Ed Dudley was battling for the lead when he came to the 13th hole. Gunning for a birdie, Dudley hit a picture-perfect drive—just as a dunderheaded spectator raced across the fairway. The ball conked the guy on the head and then bounced into the creek. As a result, Dudley made a double-bogey seven on the hole and came in third, three strokes behind the winner, Byron Nelson.

1937 Ryder Cup: A teeming crowd gathered around the 15th green at Southport, England, watching the Gene Sarazen–Percy Alliss match. Sarazen's approach shot landed in the lap of a woman—an American, no doubt—who promptly picked it up and threw it so close to the hole that Sarazen got a birdie, to go one up on Alliss and win the match on the final hole.

1954 Masters: Jack Burke Jr. was closing in on the leaders in the final round, but a heel robbed him of a chance to catch them. Only a stroke behind at the par-5 15th hole, Burke socked his second shot straight toward the green. It looked so good, he thought he might get an eagle to snatch the lead. "The green was surrounded by people, and one spectator, trying to get out of the way of my ball, fell down," Burke recalled. "My ball hit his heel and bounced clear back into the creek. I got a six, and that finished me."

1964 U.S. Open: Gary Player was accidentally pushed into a lake by adoring fans. He had just finished a practice round at Congressional Country Club when he was mobbed by spectators. "I was signing autographs, standing with my back to the lake," he recalled. "All these kids kept crowding around me, pushing me back, until they finally pushed me in. I was wearing new shoes and new pants. I just stood there in the water and kept signing."

1987 Tournament Players Championship: Jeff Sluman was tied with Sandy Lyle on the second playoff hole, an island green. Sluman looked at a five-foot birdie putt for the win. As he was about to putt, the crowd broke into cheers and laughter. The commotion was over fan Hal Valdes, who on a bet dived into the water surrounding the green. The distraction caused Sluman to step back. When he tried to putt again, he missed. One hole later, Lyle won the championship.

UNFAIRWAY MISHAPS

Golf is not the serene, quiet, pastoral game that everyone thinks it is. Quite the contrary. It can be a contact sport teeming with spills, chills, and thrills. Players have been beaned, shot, and skulled on the course. For "The Nuttiest Mishaps on a Golf Course," The Golf Hall of SHAME inducts the following:

Al Capone
Burnham Woods Golf Course, 1928

Gangster Al Capone, Public Enemy No. 1, loved to play golf. He seldom shot par—but one time he shot himself.

Although Scarface took deadly aim in the streets of Chicago, he was strictly hit and miss on the Burnham Woods Golf Course, 18 miles south of Chicago, where he often played twice a week. Usually decked out in a monogrammed white silk shirt, gray plus fours, and a belt with a diamond buckle, Capone hacked his way around the course, seldom breaking 60 for nine holes. Nevertheless, he and his fellow gun-toting duffers would play for $500 a hole.

He always kept a loaded revolver in his golf bag for protection, yet it was that very gun that wounded him. One day, while on the course, he was lifting his golf bag when one of the clubs jarred the trigger of his revolver inside. The gun went off, shooting him in the foot. Capone grabbed his injured foot, hopped around on the other, good one, and bellowed like a bull.

His bodyguards rushed him to the hospital in nearby Hammond, Indiana, but the head doctor wouldn't let him stay more than a day for fear a rival gangster, who was out to kill Capone, would shoot up the place.

Scarface was back on the links within a week, limping a little, but able to play nine holes. "After that, the boys double-checked to make sure the safety catch was on before they deposited any gun in a golf bag," recalled his former caddie, Timothy Sullivan, who was twelve years old at the time.

The golf course proved to be a dangerous place for Capone and his Chicago killers in many other ways.

"There was this crazy game Al called Blind Robin," said Sullivan in an article he wrote for *Sports Illustrated*. "One guy would stretch out flat on his back, shut his eyes tight, and let the others tee off from his chin. They used a putter and swung slow and careful. Otherwise, they would have smashed the guy's face.

"On the putting greens they'd throw down their pistol holders— clunk—and hold a wrestling match. I kept busy picking up the stuff that dropped out of their pockets—flasks, cigars, bills, and change. They made an awful mess of the greens, digging up the grass with their knees and elbows. But there was never a peep out of the management." And no other golfer who valued his life was dumb enough to complain either.

Mark Calcavecchia
1986 Kemper Open

Mark Calcavecchia, the 1989 British Open champion, withdrew from a tournament because he was too dirty.

During the rain-delayed second round of the 1986 Kemper Open at the TPC-Avenel in Potomac, Maryland, Calcavecchia's second shot on the par-5 sixth hole plopped into a deep gulley just short of the green. His ball was sitting in an inch of water because the usually dry creek bed had turned into a muddy water hazard from the previous day's downpour.

From the top of the gully, Calcavecchia looked at his ball six feet below and figured he could play it. Rather than take a long walk to where the sides of the gully had a more gentle slope, Calcavecchia elected to try the most direct route—by inching his way straight down the steep bank. This was not a wise move, considering the sides were slick and muddy.

All he took was one step down the bank, but it was a doozy. In the next instant he lay flat on his back, sliding uncontrollably feet first toward the bottom. "It was like that famous scene in *Romancing the Stone*," recalled his playing partner, Mark McCumber. Skidding down the oozy bank, Calcavecchia tried desperately to stop by flapping his arms and legs as if he were doing jumping jacks on his back. But all that did was stir up the mud on the gushy bank.

To make matters worse, Calcavecchia slid spread-eagled right into his ball, knocking it from its lie. When he finally came to a mucky stop, he found his ball wedged under his legs. By now McCumber, who was watching this mishap from the green, had fallen to his knees, weak from laughter. Even the PGA Tour officials couldn't suppress a few belly laughs. But then they turned serious and assessed Calcavecchia a two-stroke penalty for moving his ball.

With his backside, arms, legs, and hands dripping with sloppy mud, Calcavecchia staggered to his feet. "Can I at least use the water hazard to clean some of the mud off my hands?" he asked an official. Came the reply, "You can, if you want another two penalty strokes."

Wiping his dirty hands off on the few clean spots left on his mud-splattered pants, Calcavecchia took a drop and blasted onto the green. The cold, wet, filthy golfer looked like he had just stepped out of a hog wallow, yet he gamely played another three holes. But he played about as sloppy as he looked, and finally decided to do something about this mess. At the turn, he walked off the course, dumped his mud-caked clothes in the locker room, showered, and left the tournament—a sadder but cleaner man.

Ken Green and Albert Vallante

1988 U.S. Open Qualifying Sectional

Ken Green has proven he's very dangerous with a putter. Just ask playing partner Albert Vallante.

Green—the fourth-leading money winner of 1988—and his caddie Joe LaCava do a colorful routine that some players on the PGA Tour consider hotdogging. When he's walking off the green, Green flips his putter to LaCava. But these are no simple tosses. They are a series of over-the-shoulder flips and blind throws done with enough flair and flamboyance to make a band major jealous.

Most Tour players know better than to get too close to Green when he's coming off the green. But in the 1988 Qualifying Sectional for the U.S. Open at Century Golf Club in Westchester County, New York, Green was paired with Albert Vallante, a club pro from Rhode Island.

After watching Green's after-the-hole performance a few times during their first round together, Vallante paid it no further attention. He was lulled into a false sense of security because LaCava always hustled right behind Green to make the catch of the putter.

But on the 14th hole the caddie lagged too far behind. As Green came off the green, Vallante was mulling over his lackluster play and unthinkingly strolled right behind him. "Ken was so wrapped up trying out a new flip, he didn't know I wasn't behind him," recalled La-Cava. "He just saw a shadow and assumed it was me.

"I saw him test out the flip four times. It was going to be an over-the-shoulder-without-looking toss. The

BOB LIBBY PHOTOGRAPHY

91

fifth time he released the club and flipped it behind him while he was looking straight ahead.''

Vallante was walking with his head down when Green's putter crashed into his forehead and nose. Vallante stopped in his tracks, stunned. "He really didn't say anything at first," said LaCava. "I think he was in shock.''

Said Vallante, "It just happened so quick. One minute I'm walking off the tee, the next minute I'm getting hit in the head.'' Although it smarted, there was a bright side to this mishap. "Actually, it helped. I had been struggling at the time and this woke me up.''

Green, who apologized profusely to Vallante, took all the blame. "For some reason I thought he was Joe. I gave him the new experimental over-the-shoulder flip. It came down—a perfect ten, I might add—right off his noggin. The shaft kind of caught a little of his nose. But, hey, I inspired him.''

Unfortunately, not enough. Vallante missed qualifying by two strokes.

Curtis Strange and Caddie Mark Freiburg
1979 Jackie Gleason Inverrary Classic

Curtis Strange needed the help of skin divers to finish playing in the 1979 Jackie Gleason Inverrary Classic.

"It's funny now, but it wasn't funny at the time," said Strange. "It was embarrassing.''

The PGA Tour's three-time-leading money winner was a young, up-and-coming player trying to make the cut for the final two rounds. As he headed for the ninth hole, his finishing hole, Strange knew if he didn't shoot par, he would have to pack up and go home.

In order to reach the ninth tee, the players had to cross a bridge over a wide canal. The bridge—which had no railings and only a low curb—was teeming with spectators. About halfway across, Strange's caddie, Mark Freiburg, tried to get around a pack of slow-moving people by jumping up on the little curb. But he slipped and lost his balance.

"I was going into the water head first when Curtis grabbed me by the left arm," Freiburg recalled. "The bag slid off my right shoulder, but I caught it by the handle. I was down on my knees and chest, my head facing the water.''

Strange dug his spikes into the side of the curb and held on for dear life as the caddie strained to maintain his grip on the golf bag. "If I hadn't caught him," recalled Strange, "he would have gone in with the bag. As I held onto his arm, I kept watching those clubs go into the water . . . poink, poink, poink.''

All the woods followed by several irons slipped from the bag one by one into the water. As the weight of the bag decreased, Strange finally was able to bring his caddie back to his feet. After getting to the other side, the pair took an inventory of the remaining clubs. Two-iron, three-iron, five-iron, and putter. The other clubs were on the bottom of the canal and out of everyone's reach.

Rattled by the mishap and nervous about making the cut, Strange teed up his ball on the 445-yard hole and grabbed for the biggest club he had left—his two-iron. He hit down the fairway. Strange knew that if his second shot found one of the bunkers guarding the green, he was finished, because he had no club left that could blast the ball out of the sand.

"I was scared to death about going into the bunker," recalled Strange. He shortened up on his five-iron and hit a decent shot to the green. Then, with the only correct club he had for the hole, he two-putted for par and made the cut.

"Curtis was great and took the incident very lightly—once he made the cut," said Freiburg. "He told me, 'Don't worry. We'll get the clubs.' A diver did jump in and get all the clubs that night except the seven-iron. Somebody went in with scuba gear the next morning and brought us the seven-iron on the first tee.

"I was extremely embarrassed about the whole thing. After that, the other caddies started calling me 'Gilligan.' "

Gary McCord

1984 Memphis Classic

The gallery at the 1984 Memphis Classic saw more of Gary McCord than either he or they wanted—when his pants split wide open and let it all hang out.

McCord, now a color analyst on CBS golf telecasts, inadvertently revealed a new side of himself after he chose not to wear any underwear on this particular day. "You have a tendency not to do your laundry on the PGA Tour," explained McCord years later. "And just before play in Memphis, I ran out of underwear. It was a real hot day and I was wearing very tight cotton pants that stuck to my skin."

Although the tournament was no skins game, McCord turned it into one on the 15th green. He bent down to line up a putt when he heard a loud rip. "My pants ripped from the seam by my belt in the back all the way under my legs to my crotch," he said. "I thought, 'Now I know how an Indian feels.' In a panic, I dropped my putter and put both hands over my caboose because I was basically buck-ass naked." Facing a tittering gallery, a red-faced McCord slowly backed away, keeping his legs tightly together.

The fastest way out of this embarrassing predicament, he thought, was to put on his rain pants as quickly as possible. So he whispered to his caddie, "Go in my bag and get my rain pants—fast!"

The caddie shook his head and said, "Gee, I'm sorry. But since it's such a hot day and there's little chance of rain, I left your rain gear behind to lighten my load."

"That's just great," muttered McCord. He turned to his playing partner and asked if he could borrow his rain pants. The sympathetic golfer agreed, and McCord breathed a sigh of relief—until that golfer's caddie admitted that he, too, had left behind the rain gear.

Now McCord was desperate. He grabbed his caddie's towel and draped it around his waist. "It looked like I was wearing a diaper," he recalled. Spotting another group of golfers on the adjoining fairway, McCord raced over to them, related his mortifying plight, and begged for help.

"Tell you what," said one of the golfers. "I'll let you use my rain pants . . ."

"Oh, thanks, man, I really appreciate it," said an ever-so-thankful McCord.

". . . But," added the other golfer, sensing a chance to profit from McCord's dilemma, "it's going to cost you twenty bucks."

At that point McCord was willing to pay any price to save himself from further humiliation. He agreed to the deal and finished the round in rain pants.

Although McCord has managed to put that episode behind him, he said, "It was not a pleasant or hygienic experience."

Patty Hayes
1984 Samaritan Turquoise Classic

Patty Hayes learned a painful lesson: "When you have a fight with a club," she said ruefully, "the club always wins."

And she had the banged-up foot to prove it.

Hayes, winner of the 1981 Sun City Classic, was tied for the lead in the third round of the 1984 Samaritan Turquoise Classic at the Arizona Biltmore Country Club in Phoenix. But then she blew a fuse on the 13th hole when her six-iron shot fell way short.

She threw the club up in the air in disgust and then, for extra emphasis, tried to kick the shaft. But her timing was off and her ankle smashed into the club head instead. "Oh, man, did that hurt," Hayes recalled. "Ping irons don't give. I kicked the hell out of it, I was so mad." She was also in such a world of hurt that she stopped play and taped an ice pack to her rapidly swelling foot.

Then she gamely limped through the final five holes before she was taken to the hospital for X-rays. "Nothing was broken, but I did have to keep it wrapped," she said.

Rather than wear pants and hide her self-inflicted injury, Hayes chose to play in shorts so everyone in the gallery could see her bandaged ankle. "If you make a stupid move, you might as well let everyone know about it," she said.

The kicking tantrum proved to be the turning point in the match. She faltered in the final round and finished second. "But I did learn to control my temper after that . . . somewhat."

Rex Caldwell

1987 AT&T Pebble Beach National Pro-Am

Rex Caldwell's caddie needed combat pay during one major tournament. Caldwell nailed his bag-toter with a ball and then skulled him moments later with a wedge.

The back-to-back embarrassing accidents occurred on the par-4 18th hole at Cypress Point during the second round of the 1987 AT&T Pebble Beach National Pro-Am. Caldwell, the sixth-leading money winner on the PGA Tour in 1983, had just pushed his approach shot into the cypress trees to the right of the green. He decided to punch a shot under a branch three feet in front of him to get back on the fairway.

Before taking his swing, Caldwell instructed his caddie, "Lost Lee" Stehle, to stand slightly behind him. Then he swung. In a flash his third shot struck a branch, bounced straight back, and slammed into Stehle's chest. "Rex had told me to hold my position," recalled Stehle, who was staggered by the blow. "Suddenly, the ball hit the branch. There was no time to react."

After checking to make sure Stehle was okay, Caldwell showed no outward emotion over the bad break which cost him a two-stroke penalty. Only after he pulled out his wedge and chipped onto the green on his next shot did he feel the impact of hitting his caddie. Caldwell's body began to tighten with frustration and anger.

"Up until then I was playing real good, and then a delayed reaction hit me over what had happened," the golfer recalled. "I asked Lee, 'What do we lie now?' And he said, 'I think we lie six.' He was leaning over the bag when I started to put the wedge back in the bag. At the last instant I slammed it down hard. The grip of the club hit the bottom of the bag and the club shot back up, out of the bag, and hit Lee in the face. It knocked his glasses off."

Stehle, who was still smarting from a shot to the chest, now was hurting from a wedge to the face, but was not seriously injured. "I didn't mean it," said Caldwell, who apologized profusely to Stehle.

To his credit, Stehle finished the hole (which Caldwell quadruple-bogeyed) and continued to caddie for him—without wearing combat gear.

Can Laughter

Nature's Call

During the 1960 World Series of Golf at Firestone Country Club in Akron, Ohio, Jim Ferree's second shot bounced off the fourth green, rolled past the spectators, and landed near two outdoor privies, one of which was occupied.

Just before Ferree was set to hit his next shot, an official pushed his way through the gallery and said loudly, "Wait, Jim. There's a man in the outhouse. He's liable to open the door just when you hit."

The crowd stared at the privy door, waiting for it to open. But at that point the outhouse occupant had no intention of making a grand exit. Instead, everyone heard a muffled voice from inside shout, "Go ahead! Hit!"

Johnny on the Spot

During a practice round at the 1975 Jackie Gleason Inverrary Classic, Lou Graham, 1975 U.S. Open winner, used a portable rest room precariously placed on the lip of a canal.

When he tried to leave, he found that the door latch had jammed. He yelled for help, but no one heard him. "Then I got this brilliant idea to step up on the seat and kick at the latch with my spikes," he recalled. "I gave a few kicks and the outhouse began teetering like a bowling pin. A fraction more and I would've gone in the water. I had visions of being featured on the evening news: 'Golfer drowns in outhouse!' My heart jumped right up in my mouth. Golf sure is a dangerous game.

"I finally got a better idea. I took off my shoe and beat the latch open. I asked [golf shoe manufacturer] Johnson and Murphy if they wanted to do an ad on how a pair of golf shoes saved a pro's life. But they wouldn't buy it."

Skirting the Issue

Pat Bradley, 1986 LPGA Player of the Year, had her skirt swiped when she visited the bathroom between nines of a match in Japan in 1975.

Bradley had taken off her skirt and laid it over the top of the stall door. When she was ready to put it back on, the skirt was gone. "I was in a panic," she recalled. "I tried communicating with the locker-room attendants, asking, 'Where's my skirt?' And they kept giggling at me. But it wasn't funny. I didn't want to get penalized for holding up play. Thank goodness they found it. An attendant had taken my skirt because she thought it had been left there by mistake."

Getting Off the Pot

At the 1967 U.S. Open at Baltusrol, a tournament official ordered workmen to move the privies from the fourth fairway to the 16th hole once the final foursome had cleared.

A truck rumbled up and four workmen hoisted the first three privies aboard. As they picked up the fourth, a scream pierced the air. They quickly lowered the john.

Suddenly the door was flung open and a female galleryite red from embarrassment fled for the sanctuary of the trees like a frightened deer.

The Dangerous Game of Golf

Earlena Adams: Adams and Margaret McNeil were all even after 18 holes in the final round of the 1980 Club Championship at Boone Golf Club in North Carolina. As they headed to the next tee to prepare for their first hole of sudden death, McNeil took a practice swing. Her club accidentally struck Adams in the left forearm and broke it. Since Adams could not continue, McNeil was ruled the winner by default.

"Champagne" Tony Lema: At the 1957 Bing Crosby National Pro-Am, Lema became so excited on the ninth hole after making a great shot that he leaped in the air—and fell 18 feet off a cliff, bruising his shins and elbows.

D. J. Bayly MacArthur: In a 1931 tournament in Rose Bay, New South Wales, Australia, MacArthur stepped into a bunker and suddenly began to sink. The golfer, who weighed about 200 pounds, struggled to escape the clutches of the bunker but couldn't. Desperately, he shouted for help as he sank deeper and deeper. Not until he was up to his armpits did he get rescued. An investigation revealed the sand in the bunker had turned into deadly quicksand!

Bert McMillan: Playing in a West of Scotland Alliance event in 1950, McMillan found his ball lodged between two rocks. So he pulled out an iron and whacked at the ball. The ball didn't move. But his club rebounded off the rocks and struck him in the head with such force that it knocked him out cold.

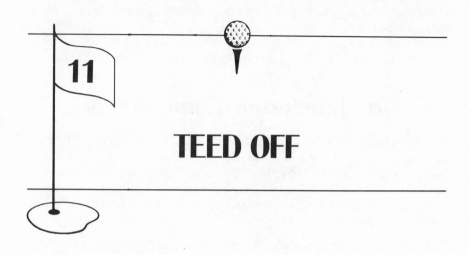

TEED OFF

The way some hotheaded players throw tantrums, they could moonlight by modeling diapers. When these guys get riled, they don't just fling their clubs and golf balls. They rant and rave and turn their conniption fits into classic histrionic spectacles. For "The Wildest Temper Tantrums Ever Thrown," The Golf Hall of SHAME *inducts the following:*

Tommy Bolt

Terrible-tempered Tommy Bolt was the Cape Canaveral of golf, the world leader in launching clubs across fairways, over greens, and into lakes. Ignited by rage, he heaved enough clubs in his day to stock a pro shop. It wasn't uncommon to see Tommy putting out with a two-iron because he had chucked his putter into the drink.

Bolt, the 1958 U.S. Open champion, threw his clubs the way he threw his tantrums—with a style all his own. His face fixed in fury, "Thunder" Bolt would rear back, plant his feet far apart for leverage and power, and hurl the offending club high in the air, making it spin like a propeller. "At one time or another," he once said, "I probably held distance records for every club in the bag."

Tommy turned club-flinging into an art form, with 40-yarders and a hang time the envy of NFL punters. He created the Bolt Dictum: "Always throw clubs in front of you. That way you don't waste energy going back to get them."

He scoffed at "flippy-wristed college kids" who tried to copy his tantrums. "I just might open a school for club-throwers," he once said, "so players could get their clubs going in the right direction and at the right angle so that the club doesn't get damaged."

Fearing that Tommy's launches were setting a bad example for the younger golfers on the tour, the PGA in 1957 adopted the "Tommy Bolt Rule" prohibiting the throwing of a club. The day after the rule was passed, Bolt rocketed his putter skyward—because he wanted to make sure he was the first fined under "his" rule.

At the 1957 Colonial in Fort Worth, Ed "Porky" Oliver saved Bolt, his playing partner, from another such fine. During the round Bolt complained about his putting and threatened to cast away his putter. On the 18th green, before 15,000 people, Tommy blew an easy putt. Porky knew that Bolt was seconds away from another angry toss, so he rambled over to Tommy, pried the putter out of his clenched fist, and threw it into a nearby pond. Then Porky burst out laughing, and so did Tommy, once he cooled down.

Club-throwing became an expensive addiction, since not all clubs were retrieved. At a tournament in the early 1950s at the Bayshore Golf Club in Miami, Bolt hooked a drive into a large lake. "Man, I was hotter than a depot stove," he recalled. "I might have parted with a finger or two, or at least three toes, before I would have given up this club. But at that moment, with the veins sticking out an inch in my neck, I was intent on getting this dude airborne." He hurled his club into a nearby canal, trying to throw a skimmer that would skip to the far bank. But this one sank. "After the round I hired a diver to try to get it for me. He couldn't find it. I let him dive $75 worth, paid him off, and called it quits."

Bolt's penchant for losing or busting clubs led to the strangest bet in golf history. At the 1953 Tournament of Champions in Las Vegas, Bolt yipped a four-foot putt and broke his putter with an irate toss. Two holes later, after driving into the rough, he smashed his driver to pieces with another mad throw. Since rules forbid replacing broken clubs, Bolt finished the round with 12 clubs, putting with his two-iron and driving with his two-wood. The next day bookies took bets on Bolt, not whether he'd finish first, but whether he'd finish the round with fewer than the regulation 14 clubs in his bag. The odds were 6–5 against Bolt. Those who took the bet followed him around the course. They thought they'd won when, after messing up a chip shot, he slammed down his iron. It bounced three feet in the air but didn't break.

"Actually, I was always more of a breaker than a thrower—most of them putters," he once said. "I broke so many of those, I probably became the world's foremost authority on how to putt without a putter."

If he wasn't flinging clubs, Bolt was abusing them in other ways—often with embarrassing results.

Once, after a bad drive, he stomped on the head of his driver. The spikes had gone so deeply into the head that he couldn't pull the club off his shoe. The players and fans were moving down the fairway and there was Bolt, back behind the tee, wearing his golf club for a right shoe.

"I choked," Bolt recalled. "I could see the next group coming up to the tee and finding me lying there with this club fixed to my shoe. I yelled, 'Hey, help me! Help me!' One of the players rushed back. He thought I'd had a heart attack. All he could see was me lying there trying to kick that club off my foot. The player soon discovered what was wrong. He snatched the club off my foot. As we walked down the fairway, hurrying to catch the other players, I noticed he was giving me plenty of room. . . ."

At least Bolt's tantrums flashed like lightning; they weren't long, drawn-out histrionics. For example, at a 1954 tourney in Virginia Beach, Bolt double-bogeyed the last hole to lose by a stroke. He stormed off the green, past the clubhouse, and right to his car, refusing to wait for his check. When tournament officials asked him to stay for the presentation, Bolt snarled, "Presentation? If you promise to present me a punch in the mouth, I'll stay. Nobody wants to see a guy who finished second." He roared off in his car and drove 15 miles before he pulled off his golf shoes.

At the 1967 Cleveland Open, during the last round, his drive on the 12th hole appeared to go into a creek that cut across the fairway. "Did the ball go in the water?" he called out to spectators. When someone answered yes, Bolt wheeled around and stalked back to the clubhouse. Had he not picked up, and instead stayed calm, he would have learned that the ball had in fact not reached the water. Bolt was two over par at the time. Those golfers who finished the tourney two over par picked up a decent paycheck.

Bolt once quit in the middle of the 1962 Philadelphia Classic because he didn't feel the crowd appreciated him. On the par-3 12th hole, he hit a beautiful shot that curved out over the water and landed ten feet from the pin. For some reason the gallery stood mum.

"Caddie, are those real people or is that just a painted Hollywood scene?" Bolt asked in a voice tinged with irritation.

"Those are real people, Mr. Bolt," the caddie responded.

"I didn't see any hands doing this," said Bolt, clapping in slow motion. Then he snarled, "If that isn't good enough, go pick up my ball. They're not going to see old Tommy hit another one." With that, he stormed off the course.

Only Tommy Bolt has ever flown into a rage *before* he muffed a putt. Once, during a Masters Tournament, his approach shot landed 30 feet wide of the flag stick on the first hole. Lining up the putt with great deliberation, Bolt began to seethe as he studied the torturous rolls of the green. He turned away, walked to the fringe, and slammed his putter to the ground. Then he missed his putt by a mile.

Perhaps no tirade of Bolt's gets talked about as much by his colleagues as the time he blew a short putt that cost him several thousand dollars. After chewing the grip off his club, he turned skyward and vented his rancor at God.

"Me again, huh?" Bolt thundered. "Why don't you come down here and play me? Come on, come on! You and your kid, too! I'll give you two a side and play your low ball!"

Clayton Heafner

Clayton Heafner was the angriest man in golf.

He never met a gallery or a course that he didn't hate.

A giant of a man with a shock of reddish hair and thick eyebrows frozen in a furrow, Heafner left a trail of pitched and smashed clubs on the PGA Tour in the 1940s.

He exploded at the slightest provocation, dishing out stinging insults to

playing partners, tournament officials, and spectators. He lunged into galleries to berate those who dared say anything critical to him. And he was always looking for a reason to quit. He picked up more times than a mother in a household of sloppy kids.

Once when a radio announcer asked golfing great Jimmy Demaret which player on the Tour had the most even disposition, Demaret answered, "Clayton Heafner."

"Heafner!" the announcer said incredulously. "Are you kidding?"

"No," replied Demaret. "He's mad *all* the time!"

Heafner directed most of his rage at the golf course itself—often before he even arrived at the clubhouse. On his way to a tournament, he thought about all the indignities to which the course would subject him—the putts missed because of rock-hard greens, the unraked sand traps, the bad lies

102

in the overgrown fairways. By the time he arrived, he despised the course. Then he cornered officials and read them the riot act about their course, which he claimed "must have been designed in Hell."

No matter how prestigious the tournament, Heafner cursed it. He was so peeved at the course at the 1940 U.S. Open in Cleveland that he picked up—before even finishing the first round. As he stalked off the course, he bellowed, "This Canterbury course is so lousy it's one godawful unplayable lie!"

Heafner holds the record for quitting without playing a single shot. He picked up on the first tee because his name was incorrectly pronounced over the loudspeaker.

When he arrived at the first tee of the 1941 Oakland Open, he heard the announcer say, "Ready to tee off is Clayton Heefner from Linville, North Carolina. Let's hope Heefner isn't going to have the same trouble with Oakland's trees that he had the year before." The spectators chuckled, remembering that at the previous tourney, Heafner had to climb a tree to hit his ball from the fork of a branch.

When the announcer finished the introduction, Heafner, his face fire-engine red, stormed over to him and snarled, "My name's Heafner, not 'Heefner.' I come from Charlotte, North Carolina, not Linville. And as for staying out of your goddamn trees, I'm not allowing myself the chance to get into them." He ordered his caddie, "Stick my stuff in my car." Then Heafner hopped into his car and roared out of town.

When things went wrong, Heafner blamed everyone but himself. After falling from second place to 16th in the final round of the 1939 U.S. Open, Heafner stormed into the clubhouse and lashed out at everything in sight: the applause from the distant galleries was too loud and distracting, the sun was too bright, the greens were too fast, his playing partners were too slow, his caddie gave him the wrong yardage.

Heafner viewed galleries the way he viewed bunkers—golf would be so much better without them. Once, in a tournament in Florida, he hit a monstrous 290-yard second shot that skipped between two bunkers and rolled onto the green. When Heafner reached the green, a heckler shouted, "Boy, you sure were lucky there. You couldn't make that shot again in a thousand years!" The hot-tempered golfer glowered at the man but didn't say a word. After holing out, Heafner calmly walked into the gallery, grabbed the heckler by the neck, and hissed, "If you so much as say one more word to me, I'll shove this ball down your goddamn throat!"

At another tournament, Heafner couldn't find the fairways with a map and compass. After sending yet another shot into the rough, he decided he'd had enough. Heafner ordered his caddie to pick up the ball. A little lady stepped out of the gallery and admonished him, "You can't just quit in a tournament like that. Where's your sportsmanship? Where's your duty to try your best? You shouldn't pick up that ball."

Heafner squinted at her and nodded his head. "You're absolutely right, ma'am," he said sweetly. Then, turning to his caddie, he growled, "Don't pick it up. Just leave the goddamn thing there!'' And he strode off to the clubhouse.

Even when a spectator cheered him on, Heafner got mad. During the 1941 Masters Tournament, Heafner was set to make a chip shot when someone in the gallery shouted, ''Get in there and pitch, Clayton, old boy. I've got five bucks on you.''

Heafner exploded. ''I'm shooting for $1,500 for myself and I should 'get in and pitch' for you and your five lousy bucks? You're crazy!''

Ky Laffoon

Touring pro Ky Laffoon treated his clubs as if they were demons from Hell, punishing them for every sliced drive and torturing them for every rimmed putt.

Laffoon, a Depression-era golfer, was the first pro to average under 70 strokes in a full season on the Tour. As a tobacco-chewing, hotheaded part-Indian nicknamed ''the Chief,'' Ky played with fire and ire. He was prone to loud clothes and even louder invectives.

Laffoon focused most of his anger on his clubs, which he brutalized in ways more suited to the Spanish Inquisition. He drowned putters, hanged drivers, and dragged irons behind his car.

At the Jacksonville Open, for instance, Laffoon became so frustrated with his putting that after walking off the 16th green, he began choking his putter. Then, still squeezing it at the neck of the shaft, he trod ankle-deep into a creek, shoved the club under the water, and screamed, ''Drown, you poor bastard, drown!''

Whenever he played a bad round, he blamed it on his clubs for letting him down. If his disenchantment with a certain club got the best of him, he dealt it a special punishment—a ride to oblivion.

''One time Ky just putted terribly in a tournament,'' recalled Sam Snead. ''Ol' Ky was so mad at his putter that he tied it to the back of his car and dragged it the whole way to the next tournament, four hundred miles away. When I asked him why he did it, he said that his putter deserved to be humiliated because of the way it behaved. So it bounced along back there for hundreds of miles, and when we finally arrived, there was nothing left but a jagged shaft.'' (Before his death, Laffoon disputed the story. ''It was a wedge,'' he said. ''I was just trying to grind the edge.'')

Another time, at the South Central Open in Hot Springs, Arkansas, Laffoon blew a fuse over heeling a ball with his driver. Shaking his club in a death grip, he raved, ''If you can't hit the ball straight, then you should hang!'' With that said, he flung the club up high into a tree, where it stuck in the fork of a branch. Once he simmered down, Ky tried to rescue the driver by throwing two more clubs up, hoping to knock it down. But they got stuck, too. Since he was playing with only seven clubs, he didn't have enough to finish the round.

Laffoon, who always played with a huge wad of tobacco stuffed in his cheek, spewed out a steady stream of juice throughout each round. The amount he spit was in direct proportion to the rise of his temper. Whenever he suffered a bad hole, he doused the bottom of the cup with a gush of tobacco juice—after first removing his ball. The player putting next would then have to reach for his ball very gingerly.

Playing partners stood clear of Laffoon when he began smoldering in anger, because he'd zap them with tobacco juice. Harry Cooper made the mistake of wearing an all-white outfit when he beat Laffoon in a playoff at the 1934 Western Open. By day's end, Cooper's pants were freckled with brown.

If tobacco juice wasn't pouring out of his mouth, ear-stinging foul language was during his flashes of rage. The intensity of his tirades embarrassed his wife Irene, who once threatened to leave him if he didn't curb his volatile temper. So Laffoon promised her that golf would no longer trigger a tantrum. At the next tournament, Ky seemed like a new man, totally in control, through nearly two rounds. But then his drive on the 15th hole landed in a bed of honeysuckle. After three futile swings, Laffoon let loose like a burst dam, unleashing a torrent of swear words that had spectators blushing as far away as the clubhouse. That's precisely where Irene, with her hands over her ears, was headed. Laffoon raced after her, and when he caught up with her, he said in a pleading voice, ''I wasn't cussing about golf, darling. I just hate honeysuckle.''

His temper caused one of the most bizarre putts in PGA history. He needed three putts from five feet to win the Cleveland Open on the last hole. But both his first and second putts lipped out of the cup. Instead of tapping in a two-incher for victory, Laffoon exploded. Not caring whether he finished first or out of the money, he slammed the putter down on the ball. Had he hit it just a small fraction of an inch to either side, he would have knocked the ball off the course. But he hit it exactly flush on top. The ball jumped two feet in the air—and plopped straight in the hole!

Greg Norman

1987 Kemper Open

Greg Norman will never be mistaken for a beanball pitcher, although there are similarities. Both have nailed opponents in the gut with a pitch. Only Norman drilled his man by accident when he lost control of his temper.

"That was probably the most embarrassing moment I ever had on a golf course," confessed the Shark, the Tour's 1986 leading money winner and British Open champion.

Playing in the first round of the 1987 Kemper Open at the TPC-Avenel in Potomac, Maryland, Norman missed a five-foot birdie putt. Since it was one of several short putts that refused to drop, the fuse on his temper was lit. After tapping the ball in, Norman angrily picked it up and felt this strong urge to vent his fury.

UPI/BETTMANN NEWSPHOTOS

Seeing the pond next to the green, Norman figured it was the perfect place to pitch his ball. Unfortunately, he didn't see playing partner Fred Couples, who was bending down to mark his ball. "I started to throw the ball into the pond," Norman said later. "Then I thought, 'No, no, no, don't do that. You'll look like an idiot.' " But his arm already was in motion.

Just as he completed his follow-through, he saw Couples. "There's Freddie marking his ball. He looks at me. I look at him . . . Geeze, I felt like a horse's ass." Norman's fast ball hit Couples right in the chest.

"I didn't know what hit me," Couples recalled. "It didn't sink in that he threw his ball. And believe me, he threw it hard. I just didn't see it coming. I was lucky he didn't hit me on top of the head. I do remember him saying, 'Oops!' "

Norman apologized to Couples, who took the incident in good humor— even though Couples missed an easy three-foot putt.

"I don't think the incident bothered Greg, because he ended up birdieing seven of the next ten holes," said Couples. "I didn't dare say anything to him or complain. He's a lot bigger than I am."

Lefty Stackhouse

Touring pro Lefty Stackhouse, as his name implies, was a raging inferno, belching a red-hot fury so uncontrollable that he blew his stack with every hook and slice.

Fortunately for his playing partners and the gallery, Lefty vented his wrath on only two things—his body and his clubs. Especially his body.

He made golf a contact sport, inflicting hell-fired pain on himself with a punch to the jaw, a kick to the shin, a club to the hand. By the 19th hole, Stackhouse looked like a victim of a back-alley mugging.

And when he wasn't rabidly assaulting his body, he was irately turning his clubs into kindling or iron pretzels.

A lean, mean golfing machine out of Sequin, Texas, Stackhouse left a trail of blood, bruises, and broken bones on the Tour during the late 1930s and early 1940s. In one of his all-time great explosions, at a tournament in Texas, Lefty placed his hand on the ball washer and violently beat his fingers with his putter until he busted several bones.

"One time when he missed a short putt, Lefty punched himself right in the jaw with an uppercut," recalled former pro Ken Venturi. "He hit himself so hard, he fell to his knees. Then he hit himself again and knocked himself out! Another time he missed a putt and took his putter and smashed it over his right hand. Now his right hand was all bloody, but Lefty wasn't finished. He took the putter in his bloody right hand and said to his left hand, 'And you're not going to get away with it, either,' and hit that hand!"

If Stackhouse socked a bad hook because he used too much power in his right hand, he'd glare at his hand as if it were disembodied and whack it against a tree while shouting, "Take that, you bastard of a hand! That'll teach you!"

Stackhouse was known, in a fit of unbridled rage, to leap head first into a hedge of thorns and thrash until he was impaled and bleeding. After shooting an 80 in a tournament at Memorial Park in Houston, Lefty worked himself into such a frenzy that he jumped into a big arbor of prickly rose bushes. There he lay, sprawled spread-eagled and face first on a bed of sharp thorns like an Indian fakir. His stunned playing partners offered to help him from his self-imposed crucifixion, but Stackhouse moaned, "Lemme be, goddamn it. Lemme stay right where I am." And so they did.

At another tourney in Louisiana, Stackhouse erupted after hooking four straight shots into the woods. He stormed over to a sturdy hackberry tree and began throwing solid right-hand punches to the tree's solar plexus while shouting, "Take that you sonofabitch! That'll teach you to mind your own goddamn business and stay the hell out of my shot!" Then, cradling his throbbing, bleeding hand, Stackhouse picked up and sought solace in the bar.

Besides his body, his clubs also bore the brunt of Lefty's blazing temper. Not a year went by during his prime that he didn't destroy an entire set of clubs, one after another, and then go after his golf bag, clawing and ripping at it until it was shredded. Often, when he failed at a crucial shot, he found a tree stump off in the rough and, starting with the driver and working down, tried to beat the stump into pulp. His clubs wound up twisted and bent like branches off a gnarled old tree.

Stackhouse was always trying to borrow a set of clubs because his were "in the shop." But those who knew Lefty didn't dare loan him their sets of clubs, not if they ever wanted to see their sticks again.

Fellow hothead Ky Laffoon recalled what happened after one kind but unaware golfer loaned his clubs to Stackhouse: "Lefty sat cross-legged in front of a fire with every wooden-shafted club he had in his bag. He'd turned them into kindling. And the guy who loaned him the sticks was standing over Lefty and chewing him out like you never heard before."

Then there was the time at the New Orleans Open when a sporting goods salesman foolishly agreed to let Lefty try a new set of clubs in a practice round. Hours later Stackhouse returned with his golf bag slung over his shoulder. He told the salesman, "I tried your clubs, but I don't think they're quite right for me." Then he turned his golf bag upside down and dumped out the new clubs—or, rather, the remains of the clubs. Each shaft had been broken in foot-long pieces.

Among the things that never failed to trigger a tirade was the water hazard. One time, at a minor tournament in Texas, Lefty belted six straight balls into a lake, playing himself clear out of the money. Exasperated beyond belief, he hurled his club into the water. Still irate, he tore his bag from the hands of his startled caddie and threw that into the lake, too. When his caddie started to giggle, the enraged Stackhouse grabbed him and threw *him* in the drink. Then, to cap off his tirade, Lefty jumped in himself.

Jim Ferree

1961 Canadian Open

Few golfers have gone over the edge quite like Jim Ferree. He decided to chuck it all in the middle of a tournament. But instead of throwing in the towel, he threw in his bag and clubs—off a bridge.

Ferree flipped out during the 1961 Canadian Open at Niakwa Golf Club in Winnipeg, Manitoba, Canada, where he was playing with Johnny Pott and Dave Marr, then chairman of the players committee. In a driving rain, a weary, aching Ferree three-putted from 15 feet on the ninth hole. The fury within him began to build by the tenth fairway.

As he walked across a bridge that spanned a creek near the front of the green, Ferree cursed his poor putting, the awful weather, a nagging backache, and his fatigue from playing in 11 straight tournaments without a break. Suddenly he stopped in the middle of the bridge.

"That's it! I've had it!" he shouted, clasping his hands on his head. "Hey, caddie, let me see my bag." His caddie warily handed it over to him and then stepped back, knowing full well this human volcano was about to explode. Then in one swift motion, Ferree pitched his club-laden bag over the railing. It was supposed to splash in the water. But his aim was off. The bag smacked into the mud. An embedded lie.

"What do we do now, Jim?" his caddie asked cautiously.

"Just leave 'em," Ferree growled.

Seeing the flying clubs, Marr rushed over to Ferree and said, "Goodness gracious, Jim! What have you done?"

"I quit!" thundered Ferree.

"No, man, you can't do that," Marr contended. "There's a $250 fine for quitting. And it's $100 for throwing a club." He peered over the railing and counted all the clubs that had spilled out of the bag and into the mud. "I don't know what they'll fine you for that."

Ferree did some quick calculating and realized that his tantrum could cost him $1,650 in fines. So he sent his man down into the mud to fetch his sticks and clean them off.

Once he cooled off, Ferree agreed to play on, and to everyone's surprise—including his own—he birdied five of the next eight holes. But his happiness and good fortune vanished on the final hole, after he hooked his drive into a rhododendron bush. With his ball resting on a waist-high branch, Ferree took a swipe at it and ticked it off a small birch tree and into another bush. The old rage resurfaced.

"Then I went crazy," he recalled. "I just started thrashing around until I wound up with a 12."

Adding to his misery, Ferree was fined $200 for his outrageous behavior. "Back then I had a bad temper," admitted Ferree, ninth-leading money winner on the 1985 Senior PGA Tour. "There was a lot of club-throwing, bag-breaking, and teeth gnashing. I guess you could say I lived in the high fine district."

Bobby Jones
1921 British Open

The great Bobby Jones, known for his cool demeanor on the golf course, used to be a young hothead who lost his temper more times than his ball.

During the 1921 British Open, his temper was tested. It failed. Jones flew into such a rage that he flat out quit—the first and only time the legendary golfer ever picked up at a major tournament.

Back then it was no big surprise. Jones was known as an impulsive nineteen-year-old upstart who threw tantrums on most every course he played. He tossed clubs toward the heavens and snapped shafts over his knee. Said Scottish pro Alex Smith in 1915, "It's a shame, but Bobby will never make it as a golfer—too much temper."

At the 1916 National Amateur Championship, Jones blew up after his competitor made outstanding shots to halve three straight holes. "I remember exactly how I felt as I walked toward the ninth tee," he said years later. "I thought I had been badly treated by luck. I had been denied something that was rightly mine. I wanted someone to sympathize with me, and I acted like the kid that I was. I didn't half try to hit the next shot, or any other after that."

A year later at a tournament at Brae Burn Country Club, Jones shocked the gallery with his volatile temper. After shanking a shot, he started heaving clubs and balls as far as he could. "I saw the blood climb his neck and flood his face," recalled playing partner Alexa Stirling Fraser, the 1916 U.S. Women's Amateur champion. "The crowd gasped in shock, and I wanted the ground to open up and let me sink from sight because I was so embarrassed for him."

But Jones's worst flare-up came, of all places, at prestigious St. Andrews, site of the 1921 British Open. He had made a brilliant showing in the first two rounds. But in the third round he was rattled by the galelike winds screaming in from the sea. He shot 46 on the front nine, a score so abysmal that his blood was boiling.

After taking a six at the tenth hole, Jones was sizzling mad, and his temper nearly reached the meltdown stage when he dumped his tee shot on the 11th hole into a bunker. He tried blasting out of the bunker four times, but each time the ball rolled back. That did it. Jones exploded. The infuriated golfer snatched up the ball from the bunker, stuffed it in his pocket, and stomped over to the edge of the Eden River. Then he whipped out his scorecard, ripped it into a dozen little pieces, and tossed them into the water.

"The English were aghast," said Fraser. "Withdrawing from a tournament was simply not done."

Back home, Jones's critics pulled no punches. Sportswriters branded him a "spoiled brat" and a "sorehead." Humiliated by the attacks, Jones saw the error of his ways and never let his temper cause him embarrassment again.

Albert Haddock

Mellion Golf Course, Cornwall, England, 1931

Amateur golfer Albert Haddock threw such a conniption fit on the golf course that he was arrested and charged with four hundred counts of swearing. But he beat the rap in court with an astounding defense—he proved that no man is a gentleman when he is playing golf!

Twice each year Haddock played Mellion, a course in Cornwall on the extreme southwestern coast of England. He usually played well until he reached the 12th hole, which featured a tee shot across an inlet of the sea bordered by cliffs 60 feet high. Known locally as the Chasm, this intimidating abyss never failed to catch Haddock's tee shots.

The Chasm played a devious mind game with Haddock. For years, every time he teed off on the 12th, he'd smack six or seven balls into the sea, then indignantly abandon the hole. At best he'd hit a shot to the boulder-strewn beach below, where he'd then flail his way back to high ground.

Haddock's infuriating misadventures with the 12th became so notorious that local citizens gathered on the cliff to watch his indomitable struggles, ultimate failures, and ranting outbursts. Then came that fateful day in 1931 when his semiannual Chasm calamity got him in trouble with the law and into court before a magistrate. Here's a contemporary account of what happened:

"On the date of the alleged offense, a crowd of unprecedented dimensions collected, but so intense was the defendant's concentration that he did not observe their presence. His ball had more nearly traversed the gulf than ever before; it struck the opposing cliff but a few feet from the summit, and nothing but an adverse gale of exceptional ferocity prevented success.

"The defendant therefore, as he conducted his customary excavations among the boulders of the Chasm, was possessed by a more than customary fury. Oblivious of his surroundings, conscious only of the will to win, for fifteen to twenty minutes he lashed his battered ball against the stubborn cliffs, until at last it triumphantly escaped.

"And before, during, and after every stroke, he uttered a number of imprecations of a complex character which were carefully recorded by an assiduous caddie and by one or two of the spectators. The defendant says that he recalls with shame a few of the expressions which he used, that he has never used them before, and that it was a shock to him to hear them issuing from his own lips; and he says quite frankly that no gentleman would use such language."

Haddock was arrested and charged under the Profane Oaths Act of 1745. For those found guilty under the act, a fine of one shilling was to be assessed to day laborers, soldiers, or seamen for each profanity, and five shillings for every person "of or above the degree of gentleman." Since Haddock was charged with mouthing about four hundred swear words and was considered a "gentleman," he faced a potential fine of 100 pounds (about $180 by today's standards).

But Haddock wasn't about to stand still for a gentleman's rate of five shillings a swear word. He admitted his guilt, but contended that the fine was excessive and wrongly calculated on the grounds that he had never been a gentleman when playing golf.

The sport, Haddock claimed, created circumstances that "will break down the normal restraints of a civilized citizen" and inflame powerful passions similar to those of a husband catching his wife in bed with another man.

According to an account of his defense, "evidence had been called to show the subversive effect of [golf] upon the ethical and moral systems of the mildest of mankind. Elderly gentlemen, beloved by children . . . are found in lonely corners of the downs, hacking at sand pits or tussocks of grass, and muttering in a blind, ungovernable fury elaborate maledictions that could not be extracted from them by robbery or murder. Men who would face torture without a word become blasphemous at the 12th hole.

"It is clear that the game of golf may well be included in that category of intolerable provocations which may legally excuse . . . behaviors not otherwise excusable, and that the gentleman may reasonably act like a lunatic or lout respectively, and should legally be judged as such."

So how did Haddock finally make out in court? A sympathetic judge ruled that the reason for Haddock's rage—the Chasm—was "exceptional" and hadn't been contemplated by the framers of the Profane Oaths Act. Furthermore, said the judge, had golf been popular at the time the act was written, "I have no doubt that it would have been dealt with under a special section."

Ruling that the case was therefore not governed by the act, the judge said, "I find that the defendant . . . was not . . . responsible for his actions or his speech and I am unable to punish him in any way. For his conduct in the Chasm, he will be formally convicted of Attempted Suicide while Temporarily Insane, but he leaves the court without a stain upon his character."

Just One of Those Flings

One day in 1952 at Hillcrest Country Club in Los Angeles, actors George Gobel and Jack Albertson invited a stranger to play golf with them.

The newcomer possessed a terrible temper, and whenever he hit a bad shot, he hurled his club in disgust. Gobel couldn't believe how far the clubs flew.

Toward the end of the round, Gobel shanked a shot so badly that he was fit to be tied. To vent his anger, he stormed over to the stranger's bag, whipped out a club, and flung it into the rough.

"Why in the hell are you throwing my club?" the guy screamed in outrage.

"Because," Gobel explained, "your clubs are used to it."

Trashing the Putter

Barb Thomas was so frustrated with her putting after nine holes of the second round of the 1986 Konica San Jose Classic that she pitched her putter into a trashcan—and lost it.

She had expected her caddie to fish the club out, but he hadn't been watching. Neither realized it was missing until they reached the next tee. Her caddie ran back to retrieve the putter, but it was gone. Apparently, a fan had grabbed it for a souvenir.

Thomas tried putting with long irons on the back nine with little success and shot a 43. Then again, she had carded a 42 on the front nine *with* the putter.

UNCONSCIONABLE LIES

Golf balls are like rambunctious little boys—they tend to misbehave and get into places they don't belong. Errant shots have taken flights of fancy that crash-landed in everything from women's bras to hot dogs; from jacket pockets to donkeys' ears. For "The Craziest Shots of All Time," The Golf Hall of SHAME *inducts the following:*

Capt. Alan B. Shepard
The Moon, 1971

Golf's first space shot was chili-dipped . . . and the second was shanked.

With two out-of-this-world swings, astronaut Alan B. Shepard holds the distinction of being the moon's first and only golfer . . . and the shame as the moon's first and only duffer.

Shepard, a 12-handicapper back on Earth, wanted to be the first man on the moon to hit a golf ball. So for the Apollo 14 space flight in February 1971, he stowed away a modified six-iron club head and two golf balls.

When all the work on the moon was completed, Shepard attached his custom-made club head to a shaftlike device that had been used by the crew to collect lunar dust samples. Then he returned to the lunar surface to play a little golf.

It was a golfer's worst nightmare. The moon is one big sand trap. Shepard was unfamiliar with the course, which was dubbed the Fra Mauro Country Club, named after the region on the moon where Apollo 14 had landed. To make matters worse, he couldn't grip the club with two hands because of his bulky space suit. He was forced to swing the club with only his right hand.

Nevertheless, Shepard had visions of scoring a crater-in-one. He had dreams of whacking a golf ball farther than anyone in the history of mankind. He was counting on the moon's reduced gravity, which is only one sixth that of Earth's. He knew that his ball would travel six times farther on the lunar surface than it would back home in Houston at the River Oaks Country Club where he played golf.

Taking his stance on the lunar surface in a gleaming white but cumbersome space suit, Shepard placed a golf ball in the fine moon dust. A TV camera beamed fuzzy pictures of him back to Earth 240,000 miles away for a worldwide audience to watch this historic moment—the first extraterrestrial golf ball ever struck by man.

Shepard took a deep breath and whipped his makeshift club with a lusty one-handed swing—but the club hit the ground before smacking into the ball. He had chili-dipped it! "You got more dirt than ball that time," laughed Commander Edgar Mitchell, who was standing beside him. However, thanks to the moon's reduced gravity, the ball still managed to sail nearly 200 yards. On Earth the ball would have fluttered no more than 35 yards.

"That ball went miles and miles and miles," Shepard shouted to Mission Control in Houston. (Later, shortly after his return to Earth, Shepard was challenged by the press over his exaggeration. "Sure I said 'miles and miles,' " he admitted. "But you know how golfers are.")

NASA

Shepard took a Mulligan and tried to redeem himself by playing his second and last ball. Again he dug up the lunar dust and again he mishit it, only this time he badly shanked his shot. The ball went no more than 50 yards—which would have been about eight yards on Earth. There were no exaggerations or excuses from him on this shot. "A ball won't hook or slice on the moon because it has no atmosphere, so this was a pure shank," he admitted.

When the golfing astronaut returned home, he received accolades for the successful completion of the space mission. He also received a slight slap on the wrist for his golfing. The Royal and Ancient Golf Club of St. Andrews in Scotland sent him the following message: "Warmest congratulations to you on your great achievement and safe return. Please refer to *The Rules of Golf* section on etiquette, paragraph 6: 'Before leaving a bunker, a player should carefully fill up all the holes made by him therein.' "

Mathieu Boya

Porto-Novo, Benin, Africa, 1987

In the wildest shot ever in the history of golf, Mathieu Boya single-handedly destroyed a nation's entire air force!

According to international news reports, here's what happened:

His devastating, wayward slice grounded the West African republic of Benin—and for that, Boya was thrown in jail.

Boya, a forty-two-year-old golf nut living in the capital city of Porto-Novo, had just finished his shift in a cotton processing plant when he decided to sock some golf balls. He had no money for greens fees, but that didn't matter because Benin had no golf course. So carrying a few battered clubs and some old range balls, he sauntered over to a nearby field adjacent to Benin Air Base and started swinging away.

Although Boya could hit the ball far, he sprayed his shots like a bad sneeze. On those rare occasions when the ball flew straight and true, he'd pause and daydream of being a world-class golfer. He wished that one day his name would be splashed on the sports pages throughout Africa.

In one fateful shot, Boya's wish came true—he did get his name in the sports pages of Africa. But it was for stroking a monumental slice, one that triggered a series of events that belonged in a Mel Brooks movie.

Boya's shot angled over the barbed-wire fence of the air base and rocketed high into the air where, like a heat-seeking missile, it slammed into a bird. Knocked out of the sky, the crippled bird plunged earthward toward the runway. Meanwhile, on the runway directly below the falling bird, a trainer jet with its canopy open was taxiing into position for a takeoff.

Just as the pilot was about to close the canopy, the stricken bird crashed into his helmet. The impact so shocked the pilot that he lost control of his craft. The jet veered off the runway and, as luck would have it, plowed right into the pride of the Benin Air Force—a row of four shiny Mirage jets. One by one the planes exploded in a thunderous fireball. In any developed nation this would have been a terrible accident. In Benin it was a catastrophe, because the five jets made up the country's entire air force. At least the pilot escaped serious injury.

On the other side of the fence Boya stood wide-eyed and frozen in disbelief. Like a murderer holding a smoking gun, Boya was still clutching his club when witnesses pointed to him as the man responsible for this debacle. The police immediately arrested Boya, threw him in jail, and charged him with the heinous crime of "hooliganism."

Prosecutors were willing to work out a plea bargain. They would agree to drop the charges if Boya made restitution. The bill for the destroyed airplanes was about $40 million. Since Boya made the equivalent of $275 a year, it would have taken him only 145,000 years to pay it off.

Boya chose to stay in jail. And he promised that when he got out, he'd never play golf again.

Marg McCann
Picture Butte Golf Club, Alberta, Canada, 1987

With one swing of the club, Marg McCann put a shameful damper on an entire men's golf league. In fact, her wildly misguided shot triggered a real drenching.

In 1987, Marg, a 21-handicapper, was playing with friend Peggy Irvine at the Picture Butte Golf Club in Alberta, Canada, early one evening. The women were not supposed to be on the course at that particular time because it was reserved for the club's men's league. But Marg and Peggy decided to play the back nine while the men were on the front nine.

The women's round was uneventful until the pair reached the 14th hole. Directly to the left of the ladies' tee is the pump house that controls the water system for the entire course. The small building appears out of the way. It would take an incredibly awful thousand-to-one shot to hit it.

Credit Marg with beating the odds. On a day when someone accidentally left the pump-house door open, Marg mishit her drive, hitting it low and hard into the building. The still evening air was shattered by pings, bangs, and clunks as the ball ricocheted like a pinball off pipes, valves, and pumps. Birds that had been serenely nesting inside scattered in squawking droves.

Just when the women thought they couldn't possibly laugh any harder, that nothing funnier could ever happen on the golf course, all the sprinklers on the front nine sprang to life, showering the players in the men's league.

"It was just a hoot," recalled Peggy. "Men were scurrying in every which direction. They were screaming and hollering and wondering what was going on. We didn't own up to it. Oh, no, we would have been in trouble from the men for sure."

Marg said that when she stopped laughing, she didn't know whether to run or hide. "Some of the fellows on the fairway across the way from us yelled, 'What's going on?' I didn't say anything. I was too embarrassed."

Marg has become a legend at Picture Butte. Another time when she teed off, Marg admitted, she dug up a huge divot with her tee still stuck in it. "When I returned to the clubhouse after my round, someone had nailed the divot up on the wall. Now I go to a different golf course."

Larry Mowry
1962 Los Angeles Open

Golfer Dave Stockton had this advice to players who get themselves in trouble: "The number one thing is . . . don't get into more trouble."

Larry Mowry, a young touring pro at the time, learned firsthand the hard truth of Stockton's sage words. Mowry hit an errant shot that could only be played by leaving the course. However, after making a remarkable recovery shot, he then faced an even bigger problem. A security guard refused to let him back onto the links.

At the 1962 Los Angeles Open at Rancho Park Golf Course, Mowry was playing the par-5 ninth hole, made infamous by Arnold Palmer's 12 in the previous year's Open. Mowry hooked his approach shot and watched disgustedly as the ball bounced off the green and, incredibly, stuck in a chain-link fence. Even though half the ball was considered out of bounds, the other half was in bounds and therefore could still be played. Rather than take a penalty-stroke drop, Mowry decided to play it where it lay.

He took his five-iron, threaded his way through the gallery, walked off the course, left through a spectators' gate, and trekked down Pico Boulevard to find his stuck ball. Then he slashed at the fence with his club and knocked the ball to within four feet of the pin.

Heaving a sigh of relief, Mowry walked back to the admission gate and tried to reenter the golf course when a security guard stopped him and said, "Where's your ticket?"

"I don't need a ticket," Mowry replied. "I'm playing in the tournament. I'm a contestant."

The guard didn't believe him. After all, what would a professional golfer be doing outside the golf course during a tournament? Besides, hadn't the guard been warned by his superiors to be on the lookout for impostors? Los Angeles was notorious for trendy spectators who carried irons in their hands and pretended to be pros.

"Where's your badge?" the guard asked Mowry.

"In my bag," said the golfer, trying hard to stay calm.

"Show me some identification."

"That's in my bag, too," Mowry said with clenched teeth.

"Well, it'll cost you five dollars for a ticket."

"I don't have five dollars!" snapped Mowry, as the hairs on the back of his neck began to bristle. "My wallet's in my bag!"

By now Mowry was feeling panicky, fearing that he had held up play so long he'd be penalized. Meanwhile, his playing partners were wondering if he had picked up, been kidnapped, or gone out to lunch. They were ready to call for a search party when PGA official Jack Tuthill showed up at the gate and escorted Mowry back to the green.

"Imagine being locked out of a tournament," recalled Mowry. "They thought I was just some other L.A. cuckoo walking around with a five-iron in my hand."

Hot Rod Hundley

1986 Showdown Classic Pro-Am

Former NBA star Hot Rod Hundley hit a series of tee shots so unbelievably wacky that if the Harlem Globetrotters were ever to form a golf team, they'd make Hot Rod a first-round draft choice.

"I thought I had seen it all . . . until now," declared Bruce Crampton, a thirty-two-year veteran of the PGA Tour.

Crampton, "Cowboy" Paul Dayhoff, and Hundley—team broadcaster for the Utah Jazz—were playing partners at the 1986 Showdown Classic Pro-Am at Jeremy Ranch Golf Club in Park City, Utah.

On the second tee, he swung his driver hard enough to stir up a mini-tornado. Alas, the ball dribbled only a few feet in front of the tee markers. But before the gallery could utter a chuckle, the ball—still moving because it had so much spin on it—skidded in reverse and rolled back right past Hundley's feet.

Hundley, shaking off his embarrassment, switched clubs and pulled out a three-wood. Once again he swung for the mountains, only to cold top the ball, which feebly rolled to the tee markers and died. Since he was still the farthest away of the three, Hundley walked over and tried again. He whacked the hell out of it. This time, to the open-mouthed amazement of his playing partners and the gallery, Hot Rod popped his ball straight up about 20 feet over his head.

With the coolness of a basketball player making a last-second, game-winning basket, Hundley dropped his club and stuck out his hand. The ball landed square in his palm.

"It was as if it were a trick that he had practiced all the time," recalled Crampton. "There's no way in the world you could make that happen again no matter how hard you tried."

Dayhoff said that when he saw Hot Rod catch his own popup, he could no longer control himself. "I was just dying laughing. For the rest of the day, every time I thought about it, I'd start to crack up. I still laugh about it."

Hundley, who carries an 18 handicap, had no idea he'd achieve golfing infamy. "The thing is, when I hit it, it sounded good and I was looking down the fairway to see where it went," he said. "Then I looked up. I saw the ball coming straight down so I caught it. Then I started marching down the fairway like this was nothing new. Actually, the whole thing was amazing. I couldn't believe it."

Said Crampton, "Those were three of the craziest shots from the tee that I've ever seen."

Mac McLendon

1979 Masters Tournament

Mac McLendon hit an odds-defying wayward shot that proved two things—his game was slightly askew but his psychic ability was incredibly sharp.

McLendon, winner of the 1978 Citrus Open and Pensacola Open, struggled in the first round of the 1979 Masters. He drove the ball badly, spraying shots everywhere but down the fairway. After scrambling to a 75, he confided to his wife Joan, "I'm playing so badly, I just know I'm going to hit somebody. In fact, whatever you do tomorrow [in the gallery], don't get out in front of me."

The next morning McLendon did just what he said he'd do. And Joan didn't do what he said she should do. Just as he feared, Mac hooked his drive off the first tee into the gallery—and you just know who was struck by the ball.

"Sure enough," recalled McLendon, "I hit a blue darter, a hook into the pines and the crowd. I heard this big thwack and I figured I hit a pine tree.

"As I was walking up the fairway to my ball, I noticed the crowd had gathered around a woman on a stick seat. I looked closer and I couldn't believe it. It was my wife!"

In recalling the painful billion-to-one shot, Joan said she lost sight of the ball in flight because the day was very overcast. "I was sitting on my little stick seat and the ball hit me right in the collarbone. Luckily, I had my badge on and that's what the ball hit. Still, it knocked me down to the ground. I just picked myself up and brushed myself off and tried to go about my business. I didn't want Mac to know he had hit me.''

At first McLendon didn't realize his prophecy had come true. As he walked up the fairway and noticed the crowd, his caddie pointed to Joan and told Mac, "You hit the woman in the brown coat." By then Joan was standing up and trying to act nonchalant. When Mac learned what really happened, he tried to lighten the mood. Noticing that his ball had ricocheted off his wife only about two feet, he told Joan, "Why didn't you at least get the ball back on the fairway?''

Despite the joke, McLendon was clearly shaken. He played on—but not very well—while Joan was taken to the hospital, where she learned her only injury was a bad bruise. Said Joan, "I returned to the gallery at the eighth hole and Mac came up to me and asked, 'Are you all right?' I assured him I was fine . . . but I could tell he wasn't.''

McLendon continued to shoot poorly and missed the cut. But at least he called his shot. Said Mac years later, "I had one shot that may go down in history as the most accurate shot in golf.''

Larry Ziegler

1976 Pleasant Valley Classic

When Larry Ziegler reached the final hole of the 1976 Pleasant Valley Classic, he had things pretty much in the bag—the bag *room*, that is.

Following an errant drive, Ziegler boldly tried to knock his second shot through the open door of the bag room and out the other side and onto the green. The ball sailed into the bag room cleanly but didn't make it out the other side. So, with spectators peering around the back doorway, Ziegler played it where it lay inside the bag room.

Ziegler's troubles had started even before his foray into the bag room. Playing at the Pleasant Valley Country Club in Sutton, Massachusetts, Ziegler felt the second round should have been called because heavy rain had turned the greens into swamps.

"I had just three-putted the eighth hole and I was damn mad because I knew I needed to birdie that hole to make the cut,'' recalled Ziegler, a three-time winner on the PGA Tour. The ninth hole, which was his finishing hole, was a short 360-yard par-4 dogleg. Rather than play the dogleg, Ziegler angled his stance, aimed directly at the green, and tried to drive over the trees that guard the fairway.

He walloped a strong drive, but to his dismay the ball took an incredibly wayward journey. It smacked into a big branch, then ricocheted off a cart path, bounded over the green, and came to rest at a spot where the clubhouse was between the ball and the flag stick.

"I could have taken a drop, but I was so damn mad that I didn't care," he said. "I decided to play it. I was just going to hack it around until I finished. I wasn't going to take any relief, or an unplayable lie. If I made a 25, it didn't matter."

Like gawkers at an accident, a growing crowd of onlookers hovered by Ziegler to see what he was going to do next. Both doors in the bag room of the clubhouse were open and he had a clear shot to the green. So he took out a six-iron and tried to chip a knockdown shot through the open front door. But the ball clipped a bag and zipped about the room like a ricocheting bullet. Ignoring the whispered laughter from the gallery, Ziegler held his temper in check and finally shot the ball out the door and onto the green. Then he stalked out the front door, followed by a steady flow of spectators who had streamed through the bag room.

Ziegler, who made a double-bogey six on the hole, was fined $500 by the PGA Tour for conduct unbecoming a professional. "They didn't think it was very funny," he said. "I thought it was. I got a good laugh for $500."

Crazy Shots That Guaranteed Automatic Induction into The Golf Hall of SHAME

Pro Division

Hale Irwin: Irwin tried to make the breast of a bad situation. His shot wound up in a spectator's bra! When the ball flew into the gallery at the 1973 Sea Pines Heritage Classic in Hilton Head, South Carolina, Irwin and PGA official Clyde Mangum searched around but couldn't find the ball. They were ready to give up when a red-faced woman finally spoke up and said the ball was in her bra. It had struck her high in the chest, rolled down the top of her dress, and lodged in her undergarment. "The ruling is that the golfer take the ball out [of the obstruction] and drop it," said Mangum. "However, in this case, the lady took it out."

Curtis Sifford: Sifford hit a ball that landed smack in a hot dog. At the Quad Cities Open he sliced a shot into the crowd and yelled "Fore!" Seeing the ball heading straight for her, a woman frantically dropped her hot dog and scampered out of the way. Unfortunately for Sifford the ball plopped right into her hot dog. He didn't relish the thought of what he had to do next. To the howls of laughter from the gallery, Sifford had to clean off the mustard and ketchup first before taking his drop.

Gene Sarazen: Sarazen hit a shot so perfect it was shameful. It happened at the 1936 Western Open when he was playing with Jimmy Demaret. On a par-3 where the green was surrounded by a lake, Demaret drove first. He took dead aim on the pin and dropped a beauty no more than six feet from the hole. With a cocky swagger, Sarazen stepped up to the tee and hit an identical shot—except his ball came down right on top of Demaret's ball. While Demaret's ball inched closer to the cup, Sarazen's flew into the lake. He wound up with a six. Recalled Demaret, "You never saw such a mad little guy."

Jane Geddes: Geddes won the 1986 Boston Five Classic after receiving a pocketful of help from a member of the gallery. In the final round, Geddes's tee shot on the par-3 sixth hole sailed off target and flew into the shirt pocket of a male spectator. He was unhurt because the landing was cushioned by a pack of cigarettes. Although Geddes scored a bogey on the hole, she was very lucky. The man she hit was standing near a water hazard and he had unwittingly blocked her shot from a worse fate. Geddes won by one shot.

Sam Snead: "In the Cleveland Open one year I was about to collect a few thousand bucks for first prize when my approach sailed over the green toward the locker room," Snead recalled. "The lockers adjoined the green. The ball was sure to bounce back either onto or close to the green. Just then a course policeman opened a door. The ball whizzed past his ear and stopped in the last stall of the men's toilet. The two-stroke penalty cost me the Open by one shot."

Pete Cooper: At the 1959 Western Open, Cooper dumped his tee shot into a woman's handbag. She had scurried out of the way of the ball and didn't even know the ball was in her bag. She discovered it a few minutes later when she reached in her purse for a cigarette and pulled out the ball. She returned it just in time to save Cooper from a two-stroke penalty for a lost ball.

Amateur Division

Dr. George Russell: Dr. Russell inadvertently hit his ball *backwards* 300 yards! Playing in the 1913 Braids Tournament in Scotland, Dr. Russell displayed a bizarre backswing. As he got set for a drive off the tee, he accidentally struck the ball on one of his back waggles. The ball jumped the fence behind the tee and careered down a steep hill, coming to rest over 300 yards away!

Charles Greenstone, Sr.: At the 18th hole of a club tourney played at the Lake Merced Club in San Francisco years ago, Greenstone sent a shot over the green, past an entrance road, and up a walkway to the clubhouse kitchen door. The ball bounced up toward the door just as it was opened by a cook who was holding a bowl containing two eggs. The ball landed in the bowl and cracked the eggs—for a bowl-in-one.

Michael McEvoy: McEvoy made golf's most asinine shot. At Middleton, County Cork, Ireland, in 1922, McEvoy's drive from the third tee went right into the ear of a donkey that was grazing in the fairway. The stunned ass stood still for a moment. But when McEvoy got within a few yards of the animal, it took off. About 50 yards into the rough the donkey shook his head and the ball fell out. The ball was so deep in the woods that McEvoy took a double-bogey six.

Harry Leach: Leach recorded the longest drive in golf history. But he wasn't proud of it. Playing at St. Andrews in 1954, Leach drove from the first tee as a pickup truck loaded with rubbish motored on the road that crossed the first and last fairways. The ball landed in the bed of the truck on top of the debris and wound up at the town dump a mile away.

Oscar Grimes: While attempting to qualify at the 1939 Western Open, Grimes knocked a shot into a hamburger stand. The ball hit a key on the cash register, opened the cash drawer, and dropped in!

No Parking

Long before JoAnne Carner was inducted into the World Golf Hall of Fame, she established a reputation for laughing at her mistakes.

Once, on the first hole of a tournament early in her career, she hit her first two drives into an adjoining parking lot. Rather than curse her rotten luck, she turned to the hushed gallery and announced, "Well, that lot's full. Let's see if I can park this baby someplace else."

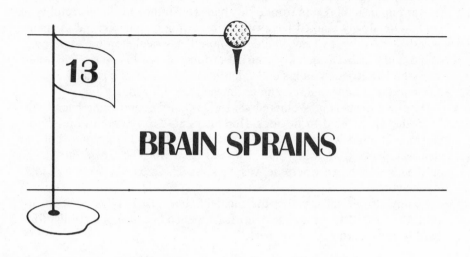

BRAIN SPRAINS

Pro golfers concentrate on every drive, every fairway shot, every putt. Baloney! These guys daydream and get lost in their thoughts just like the rest of us working stiffs. The only problem is that their office is the golf course, and when they suffer a mental lapse, it usually spells disaster. For "The Most Mind-Boggling Mental Miscues," The Golf Hall of SHAME *inducts the following:*

Roger Wethered
1921 British Open

In the most notorious mental lapse ever in the history of the British Open, Roger Wethered forgot where his ball lay and accidentally stepped on it. The resultant penalty stroke proved very costly—because without it, he would have won the 1921 Open.

"It is clear that the fates did not intend for me to win," lamented Wethered years later.

Wethered, then a twenty-three-year-old Oxford student who would become one of Britain's most famous amateur golfers, wasn't given much chance of winning the Open at St. Andrews. But he played remarkably well to keep pace with the leaders.

However, during the third round he literally stepped into trouble on the 14th hole. His ball lay in the middle of the fairway, short of the notorious Hell Bunker. "There was a large gallery on the adjoining fairway and it was impossible for me to play to the 14th green until the way was clear," he recalled. While Wethered waited for the gallery to move on, he walked forward up a small rise in front of his ball. He studied his line carefully.

Then he slowly walked backwards, forgetting for one crucial moment exactly where his ball lay. Suddenly he felt his heel step on something round and hard. He quickly whirled around to see his worst fear realized—he had trodden on his ball. That meant a one-stroke penalty . . . an infraction that he would remember for the rest of his life.

Despite the mishap, Wethered shot a 72 that day and came back with 71 in the final round to tie Jock Hutchison at 296. It was a bittersweet finish. Wethered was thrilled to have tied for the championship, but he also was peeved, knowing that he would have won the Open outright if only he had watched where he was walking. The next day Wethered lost in a playoff.

"Many people have called the incident the most famous accident in golf," he said. "It was no accident. It happened because of a straightforward lapse of memory on my part."

Walter Hagen

Walter Hagen, who won an unprecedented four consecutive PGA Championships, *had* to keep on winning—because he had lost the traveling trophy.

When Hagen won the 1924 PGA at French Lick (Indiana) Country Club, he was presented with the Fred Wanamaker Trophy, an engraved silver cup that each year's winner got to keep until the next championship. Hagen then took the cup with him to Chicago where he negotiated a contract with the Wilson Sporting Goods Company.

He didn't think about the traveling trophy until a year later, when again he won the PGA, this time at Olympia Fields Country Club near Chicago. When he was asked to bring the trophy to the official presentation, the Haig realized he had lost it. Fudging the truth, he told officials, "Sorry, I forgot to bring it with me."

A year later, at the Salisbury Golf Course on Long Island, Hagen won the PGA for the third straight time. Once again officials asked about the trophy and once again Hagen brushed them off. He told them he had it safely at home and that in his rush to get to the Championship he hadn't had time to pick it up. Since he won the tournament, officials didn't press the issue.

Before the start of the 1927 PGA at Cedar Crest Country Club in Dallas, Hagen's conscience got the better of him and he confessed. He told officials he didn't have the slightest idea where the trophy was. The last time he'd seen it was when he put it in a cab with him three years earlier in Chicago.

Hagen won the PGA for the fourth time in a row, so the question of the trophy's whereabouts was still academic. But by this time the PGA officials had given up hope of ever seeing the trophy again and were ready to have a copy made.

Then a strange thing happened. Someone poking around in the Wilson Sporting Goods warehouse in Chicago came across an unfamiliar box. The box was opened, and lo and behold, there sat the trophy.

But while the trophy showed up at the start of the 1928 PGA, Hagen didn't. Incredibly, after winning four straight PGA Championships, the Haig forgot that he was due at the tourney at the Five Farms Course near Baltimore. When he failed to make an appearance for practice rounds, officials scouted around and found an unaware Hagen blissfully playing exhibitions in Pennsylvania. After receiving a wire from the PGA, Hagen hurriedly motored down to defend his title.

Finding the trophy must have been a jinx to Hagen because he lost to the eventual winner, Leo Diegel.

The PGA has since presented each winner with his own smaller replica of the silver cup to keep. The original Fred Wanamaker Trophy remains on display at PGA Headquarters in Palm Beach Gardens, Florida, and is brought to the site of each championship. This should prevent a modern-day version of the saga "Walter Hagen and the Lost Cup."

Bobby Jones
1926 British Open

The great Bobby Jones had to pay spectator's admission in order to play in the final round of the 1926 British Open—because he forgot his contestant's badge.

It happened during a double round at Royal Lytham and St. Annes Golf Club, on England's west coast north of Liverpool. After the third round in the morning, Jones had shot 217, good for second place behind Al Watrous, who was leading with 215. The two were then paired for the final afternoon round.

Jones suggested that he and Watrous get away from the clubhouse crowds during intermission and go to his room in the nearby Majestic Hotel for a rest, a quiet lunch, and a chance to steady their nerves. After they arrived, the two removed their shoes and each stretched out on a bed and tried to relax. But both were too keyed up. In fact, they barely touched a room-service lunch of tea, toast, and cold ham.

When they returned to the players' entrance gate to the clubhouse, Watrous flashed his player's badge. But Jones was stopped by the guards, who asked to see his badge. Jones searched his pockets to no avail. Then

it dawned on him. He was so preoccupied thinking about the final round that he had forgotten his badge, which was back in his hotel room.

Surely someone recognized him, he said to the clubhouse guards. After all, he was a contender in this tournament and one of the most dominant golfers of his era, having already been on three Walker Cup teams and having won both the U.S. Open and the U.S. Amateur twice. If anyone recognized Jones, he didn't admit it.

No amount of pleading from Watrous and Jones could convince the guards that Jones was a contestant. No badge, no entry; it was as simple as that. Finally, with tee off rapidly approaching, the frustrated Jones told Watrous to go on in. Knowing he didn't have enough time to go back to the hotel and retrieve his badge, Jones figured there was only one other way to gain entrance—pay for it. So he walked over to another gate, stood in line with the spectators, and paid the common admission charge of several shillings.

Once on the course, Jones didn't need any badge to prove he was one of the world's best golfers. In the final round, he shot 74, four better than Watrous, to capture the British Open, 291 to 293.

Babe Ruth
Miami Country Club, 1934

Babe Ruth, whose passion for golf was second only to baseball (which was second only to booze, buffets, and bimbos), played with an embarrassing handicap—he seldom could remember the names of his golfing companions.

Ruth had a habit of calling his playing partners "kid," the same name he called many of his own Yankee teammates whenever he forgot their names, which was quite often.

But the Babe's forgetfulness was never more ridiculous than the day he played in a foursome at the Miami Country Club in Florida, shortly before the start of spring training in 1934. Ruth was playing golf with 1931 U.S. Open champion Billy Burke and two young assistant club pros whom the slugger had met for the first time.

After nine holes of whacking golf balls and swapping jokes, the foursome took a break and one of Ruth's playing partners walked with the Babe to the pro shop. Within seconds, caddies, club members, and children swarmed around Ruth, who, as always, was cordial to his fans. He politely answered questions and signed a few autographs.

"Hey, Babe," said a voice in the crowd. "Who are you playing with?"

"Oh, it's just a friendly little round," Ruth replied. "I'm playing with Billy Burke and a couple of palookas." He turned to a golfer who had been following him and said, "Well, kid, so long. I'll be seeing you." Then the Babe headed back toward the tenth tee.

"You will be seeing me a lot the rest of the afternoon, for I'm going with you," said the golfer. Ruth crinkled his nose and looked perplexed. "Listen, Babe," said the golfer. "You know me, don't you? Just think a minute. Where did you see me last?"

"Gee, I ought to know you," said Ruth. "Your face is so familiar that I'm sure I've met you before, maybe a lot of times, but I just can't recall where. Who are you?"

"Well, I'll tell you, since you don't remember," said the golfer with a widening grin. "I happen to be one of the palookas you are playing with this afternoon."

Beverly Hanson
1956 Peach Blossom Classic

Beverly Hanson discovered that there are times when it's better to be lost in the woods than lost in thought.

Hanson, the 1955 LPGA champion, was playing in the 1956 Peach Blossom Classic in Spartanburg, South Carolina, when she sliced her ball into a clump of trees off the fairway. Bev found her ball after a short search. Then she studied her upcoming shot, which was a tough one that had to be knocked between two trees. She was staring at her ball, trying to figure out what club to use, when her eyes focused on a golf-ball-sized rock a few inches away.

Thinking that the rock might be in the way, Bev reached down to pick it up. But because she was still totally engrossed in planning her shot, she absentmindedly grabbed her ball by mistake—and heaved it even deeper into the woods!

"I was doing such a super job of concentrating on that shot and how I was going to hit it between the trees," Hanson recalled. "That's all I was thinking about. I just picked up what was on the ground. When the ball left my fingers, I sort of thought in the back of my mind that it seemed like an awfully lightweight rock. The worst thing is that I threw the ball backwards over my shoulder, and I did it with a lot of gusto.

"I turned to [playing partner] Betsy Rawls and said, 'Oh, my God! I just threw my ball in the woods!' "

Rawls has never forgotten Bev's mental lapse. "She must have thrown it fifty yards," said Betsy. "Everybody was laughing and she was so mad. But it was really funny to us because it happened to someone else. It was the funniest thing I ever saw on the golf course."

Hanson was supposed to replace her ball in its original position and take a one-stroke penalty for moving the ball. But by then she was so rattled that she forgot the rule. Instead of replacing the ball, she played it from where the ball landed after she had thrown it. As a result, Bev incurred two more penalty strokes for playing the ball from the wrong place.

"It was the laugh of the day when we finished the round," said Hanson. "Even I found myself laughing about it. What else could I do?"

Ken Green Steve Melnyk Philip Parkin

1986 Canadian Open   1976 Hawaiian Open   1988 Provident Classic

To their chagrin, Ken Green and Steve Melnyk learned there's no way to win a tournament without first entering it. And Philip Parkin learned there's no way to win a tournament without first knowing where it is.

They were all victimized by their own brain sprains.

For the 1986 Canadian Open, Green decided to bring along an entourage. So he packed his van with his caddie, mother, sister, son, niece, and two dogs. They drove eight and a half hours from his hometown of Danbury, Connecticut, to Toronto and checked into their hotel rooms. After they were all settled in, Green asked for a pairing sheet to see his tee times.

All at once he was stricken with the sickening sensation that accompanies all sudden realizations that you forgot something real important. It dawned on Green that he had never bothered to enter the tournament! And it hurt even more when he learned that there was room for him in the tourney. But by the time he found out, it was past the deadline.

"We went to Niagara Falls the next morning and then drove back," he said. "There was nothing else I could do."

Incredibly, a year later Green screwed up another entry. He was getting ready to fly to the Greater Milwaukee Open when he called tournament officials about a hotel room. Tournament director Gordon Kress wondered why Green wanted a room. Green hadn't entered the tourney. "Obviously," recalled Green, "I didn't bother to catch my flight."

Ironically, in 1988 Green won both the Canadian Open and the Greater Milwaukee Open—after first making sure he had entered.

In 1976, years before he became a color man on CBS golf telecasts, pro golfer Steve Melnyk flew 4,000 miles to Honolulu for the Hawaiian Open . . . and the shock of his life.

"I went out to the course at Waialae Country Club on Monday," Melnyk recalled. "Jack Sterling, one of the officials, came up to me and said, 'What are you doing here?' I said, 'Playing.' And he said, 'Well, we don't have you committed.' I had made a verbal commitment to play but they needed a signed commitment sheet. It went downhill from there.

"So I flew from Pebble Beach [site of his last tournament] to Honolulu to Jacksonville, Florida, in a twenty-four-hour period. I called the Tour office and pleaded my case, but it fell on deaf ears. It was like I was speaking Arabic. It cost me $800 in plane fares. That was a lot of money for me at the time."

At least Welshman Philip Parkin never had a problem entering tournaments. His problem was *finding* them. After signing up for the 1988 Provident Classic, Parkin flew to Providence, Rhode Island, and waited for a courtesy car to pick him up at the airport. Two hours later he was still waiting. It took a phone call to find out why.

Parkin had his Providents and Providences mixed up. The Provident Classic is played not in Providence, Rhode Island, but 800 miles away in Hixson, Tennessee.

Putting His Wrong Foot Forward

During the third round of the 1953 Masters, Johnny de Forest whacked his ball into the bank of Rae's Creek in front of the 13th hole.

After carefully surveying the situation, he felt he could play the ball with one foot in the water. He pulled off his left shoe and sock and rolled his pants above the knee. Then he carefully planted his bare left foot on the bank—and, in his flightiness, stepped into the water with his right shoe!

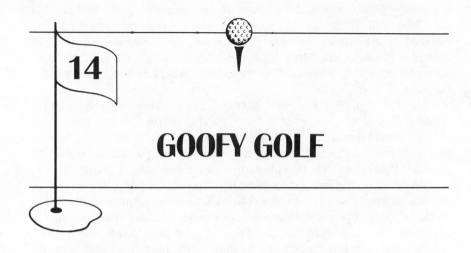

14

GOOFY GOLF

When you think of golf tournaments, you think of the majors, those distinguished Tour events steeped in prestige and tradition. But those are for the world's best linksmen. The diehard duffers, the clubhouse clowns, and the pitiful putters must play in events more suited to a sideshow. For "The Zaniest Tournaments in Golf," The Golf Hall of SHAME *inducts the following:*

Firecracker Tournament
Indian Canyon Golf Course, Spokane, Washington

In the most tumultuous, ear-splitting, earth-shaking golf tournament in the world, competitors were forced to play amid a cacophony of firecrackers, sirens, bells, and horns.

Raucous bedlam was par for the course at the Firecracker Tournament in Spokane, Washington, a wild and wacky fund-raising affair that exploded annually on the golfing scene from the 1940s through the 1970s.

For golfers it was like playing through a firefight in the streets of Beirut. The booms, bangs, and blasts startled players out of their strokes, shattered their nerves, and helped send their scores soaring as high as a Roman candle.

"With those firecrackers going off, golfers would fan on their swings or top their drives or even pop it straight up," recalled C. J. Malico, a 1976 winner. "It wasn't easy, but it was fun. There was a lot of horseplay."

Players who normally lost their concentration whenever a bird twittered never made it off the first tee. Teeing up the ball signaled a thunderous assault on the senses. Just as each player went into his swing, locomotive bells clanged, fire sirens shrieked, machine guns (with blanks) rat-a-tat-tatted. Firecrackers exploded at the golfer's feet. Bottle rockets whizzed by his ears as smoke bombs that would have hidden a battleship obscured his ball. Not content with these pyrotechnic distractions, officials parked automobiles with loudspeakers that blared music down the fairways.

Even if he survived the first barrage, the golfer was far from safe. Spectators, caddies, and even his own playing partners were encouraged by tournament organizers to launch surprise attacks, bombarding him on his backswing with cannon crackers, torpedoes, and flares. And if he survived that onslaught, he still had to face a fusillade of cherry bombs and whistlers on the final green as he tried to putt for par.

Back in the 1940s, before the Age of Lawsuits, about a million firecrackers were shot off during each tournament held at Indian Canyon Golf Course and staged by the Spokane Athletic Round Table. The organization even hired a tailor to stand by at the ready to mend the pants of any player whose trousers might get burned from a firecracker.

More than 150 amateurs from throughout the country were foolish enough to enter the tournament. It was easy to spot the cautious veterans of the tourney—they wore gas masks and even asbestos suits.

The tournament was held to "take some of the stiffness out of golf for at least one game during the year," Joseph Albi, president of the Round Table, told reporters. "It is all in the spirit of fun. We believe that most players take their game too seriously, anyhow. They're altogether too touchy about the least bit of noise—too temperamental."

That wasn't the case for those who played in the tourney every year. They were probably hard of hearing from all those deafening firecrackers.

Club-Throwing Tournament
Druid Hills Country Club, Atlanta, 1936

In a zany tournament that flew in the face of golf-course etiquette, the Druid Hills Country Club in Atlanta staged a club-tossing competition.

More than sixty contestants were free to do what they were forbidden to do on the links—heave their clubs. The golfers hurled clubs left-handed and right-handed for distance. They wowed spectators with high throws and accurate tosses, and they dazzled the judges with marvelous, unique styles.

The wacky tourney was dreamed up by Harry Stephens, the club pro. "We had several near accidents on the course because of flying irons," he explained to reporters. "One day I was reading the riot act to a youngster and as a parting shot I said, 'One of these days I'm going to put on a club-throwing contest to show you how really stupid you look.' Then the thought struck me: Why not? Maybe it would do some good."

For two days prior to the tournament, members came out to the "practice tee." Players discovered that irons were by far the best to throw, especially the putter, because it was short and heavy. During practice Stephens himself learned that flinging a club wasn't as easy as it looked. "One of the clubs I tossed sailed in the wrong direction," he confessed. "It went right back over my head and onto the clubhouse veranda. It was a good thing no one was hurt."

On the day of the tourney, held in 1936, golfers, club members, and curiosity seekers crowded around the club-tossers and cheered with the vigor of a Masters tournament. "It was surprising how many club chuckers hooked their chucks," said a news account. "There were very few slices."

Julius Hughes won the competition for altitude. He launched a pitching iron about 20 feet over the top of an 80-foot pine tree. For distance, right-hander Randolph Timmerman took top honors, heaving a club an amazing 61 yards, while Ned Roberts earned the southpaw prize for distance with a toss of 50 yards. Philip Ethridge copped the accuracy toss by hurling his eight-iron within seven feet, eight inches of a target from a distance of 50 yards.

For style, no one could beat Jesse Draper for his "combination of the conventional hammer-throw-spin and a brilliantly executed kangaroo-hop," according to a newspaper account. In his winning throw, Draper grasped the club and angrily started to break it over his knee. Then he twirled like a whirling dervish and followed that up with an Indian war dance accompanied by whoops and hollers. This flowed into a Fred Astaire–Ginger Rogers routine in which he danced as if his club were a lady partner. Draper finished his histrionics by dropping to one knee and letting the club fall gently to the ground.

The winners' throws probably weren't as dramatic as those heaved in anger, admitted Stephens. "We should have followed each of the contestants around the course during an important match and waited until he flubbed an easy shot. That's when we should have measured his throw. But conditions are rarely ideal, and the boys did the best they could under the circumstances.

"When all the events were over and it was time to make the awards, I told the winners they should be ashamed of their proficiency. But you know, the contest did more to check impulsive club-throwing than any warnings posted on the bulletin board."

Cow Chip Open

Lawrence (Nebraska) Country Club

It used to be that on the second Sunday of June, golfers let the chips fall where they may. Cow chips, that is.

For years, more than a hundred players from as far away as New York and California flocked to the tiny Nebraska town of Lawrence (population 390) to play among 50 cows and hundreds of cow plops in the world's most fragrant tournament—the Cow Chip Open.

"The hard cow chips were the worst," recalled player George Dell of Texas. "They'd knock your ball catawampus. Now the fresh ones, they weren't too bad. One time my ball was rolling right toward a bunker and it plopped into a fresh cow pie and stopped. Of course, it wasn't a whole lot of fun picking the ball out and cleaning it."

In the 1965 tourney, a player from Chicago finished the first nine holes in one over par and was bragging about how he had dodged all the cow pies. But then his low, screaming drive on the first hole of the second round struck a hard cow chip and rebounded 30 feet behind the tee. He was so shook up that he carded an 11 on the hole.

The annual tourney began in 1958, shortly after a group of local golfers founded the Lawrence Country Club. "A farmer rented them about eighty acres of land for the course, but only on the condition that he be allowed to keep his cows on it," said Allen Ostdiek, a weekend golfer and publisher of the local paper, *The Lawrence Locomotive*. "The golfers agreed, and they just got used to playing around the cows and the cow pies. I've hit a few cows and cow pies in my time."

Out-of-town players were somewhat unnerved by the nine-hole course since most had never played on greens made of sand, fairways mined with cow pies, and roughs inhabited by bossy cows. Then there were those daffy local rules. If a ball landed in a fresh cow chip, the golfer could lift his ball, clean it, and drop it within two club-lengths without penalty. If the ball hit a cow, the ball was played where it lay, assuming the cow had moseyed out of the way.

Barbed-wire fences were constructed around the sand greens to keep the cows off them. If an approach shot hit the fence, the player could hit another ball with no penalty.

Golfers from throughout the country have entered the tourney just so they could go back home and tell their friends they played in the Cow Chip Open. All have shot for the coveted trophy—a golden cow chip with a ball stuck in the middle. "They used to give the winner a real dried-out cow chip," said Ostdiek. "But those didn't last long."

The cows and their chips no longer grace the course. The country club bought the land outright in 1975 and fenced off the cows. However, the Cow Chip Open is still held on the second Sunday in June. The townspeople hope it will grow into a major tournament. But that kind of thinking is just cow pie in the sky.

SLAM Invitational

New Orleans

They come with one goal in mind—to win and proudly don the coveted green jacket. No, this isn't the traditional sports coat presented to the champion of the prestigious Masters. It's the ugly, lint-collecting, thrift-shop special given to the champion of the SLAM Invitational.

Only at the SLAM are the rules as goofy as the golfers. Players must dress as though they bought their clothes at Barnum & Bailey's. The zanier the better. They've played as Cleopatra, Hell's Angels, vamps, Indians, and soldiers.

Besides the strict dress code, other rules that you'll never find in any other tournament include: to speed play, a golfer can play the divot or the ball, whichever travels the farthest; and if there is an unplayable lie, the golfer gets a free kick or free throw. Participants play in teams consisting of a male and a female. The male is responsible for hitting the ball until it rests on the green. The female partner does the putting.

The tourney was conceived for absolutely no socially redeeming purpose. Barry "Foot-Wedge" Schully, John "Dr. Rough" Lambert III, and Bill "Humphrey Bogey" Michaelis initiated the SLAM Invitational in 1983 when they were students at Louisiana State University. (The name SLAM is an acronym of letters from their last names.)

Since it features heavy emphasis on carousing and the wearing of silly clothes, the tournament has never been invited back to the same golf course twice. Serious golfers scatter when the SLAMmers take to the course. Golf balls ricochet off oak trees, hop over greens from every direction, and fly onto other fairways. No one is safe.

"Ninety percent of the players have never hit a golf ball before," said Lambert. "But that doesn't stop anyone from having fun and trying to win." From 90 to 150 couples enter the tournament.

"At first it started out as a way of getting friends together," said Michaelis, now a veterinarian. "We had a bloody-Mary-and-screwdriver breakfast and went out and played at the university course in Baton Rouge. Then we moved it to New Orleans." Now the tournament is held whenever organizers get around to setting it up.

In the second SLAM, held at City Park's south course in New Orleans, Lambert's parents, John and Nora (see photo on next page) wowed the rest of the field with their attire. John, a former New Orleans city councilman, wore a World War II helmet, a gray bathrobe adorned with Army medals, red socks, and tennis shoes. Nora was decked out in a red

bathrobe, a brown feather boa, and a floppy hat. "Why are people looking at us?" asked Nora in feigned innocence.

One male player graced the course in a brightly flowered dress and quickly picked up the name Klinger after the dress-clad character in the TV series *M*A*S*H*. Another golfer wore a silk shirt under a leisure suit, while a buddy played in grossly oversized plaid pants held up by suspenders. Others donned Salvation Army duds.

But for sartorial kitsch, no one could match the Lamberts, who won the award for the most obnoxiously dressed couple. Other major awards included one for the longest drive—won by Chris Schully, who drove all the way from Oxford, Mississippi. Then there was the cherished Foot-Wedge Trophy, which features a gold shoe with a sand wedge driven through the toe. It goes to the player with the most improved "lies." In 1984 it went to tall-tale-teller Harry Solis.

The highest score on the par-37 nine-hole course was an atrocious 74 by the team of Jay McGuire and Missy Miller. They were far outdistanced by first-place winners John Duviehl and Jeanne Walther, who shot a three-over-par 40. Like other winning couples before and after them, they came away with much more than just bragging rights. Duviehl won the SLAM's traditional green coat (which is passed on to the next year's winner). His partner, on the other hand, won the purse. In this case the purse was a tasteless vinyl handbag with matching shoes.

International Tournament for Discriminated Against Golfers Who Don't Look Good but Would Like to Be Felt Wanted Anyhow Open

Frederick (Oklahoma) Golf and Country Club

It was by far the biggest golf tournament in the world—in name and in shame.

It was a tourney where the diehard duffer shined; where nobody cared who played well, as long as he kept quiet about it; where the typical hacker played a 6,414-yard course in 14,000-plus yards.

It was the International Tournament for Discriminated Against Golfers Who Don't Look Good but Would Like to Be Felt Wanted Anyhow Open (or the ITFDAGWDLGBWLTBFWA Open for short).

In 1967 Frank Boggs, sports columnist for the *Daily Oklahoman*, complained that a golfer had to be a par-birdie-par shooter to ever get an invitation to play in any golf tournament and that somebody ought to do something about it. Somebody did. The Frederick Golf and Country Club created the ITFDAGWDLGBWLTBFWA Open, where contestants were "laughed at, about, and with, and otherwise ridiculed through 18 holes of harebrained hilarity," according to its founders.

From 1967 through 1970, the country club set aside one Sunday a year for the "deprived" golfers of the world, those underprivileged patrons of the links, who under no circumstances would ever be invited to take part in any other kind of tournament. Consequently, the tournament required a whole set of special local rules.

Automatic disqualification went to any player having back-to-back pars. Officials said such a golfer gave himself away as nothing but a "trophy hunter." The golfer with the best score was automatically disqualified as well. But in either case, the culprit was allowed to play, so the DQ was merely a statement of principle. The rules let golfers improve their lies in the fairway, in the rough, in the sand traps, on the greens, and in the clubhouse bar. Duffers could pick up their balls and add one stroke after four-putting any green.

As an added dimension to the game, each player was given a "gotcha" coupon. Whenever another player goosed a fellow golfer, the gooser had to give the goosee the "gotcha" coupon. The player who collected the most "gotchas" won a prize.

Awards were given out for the shortest tee shot, the worst blown putt, the most whiffs on an attempted shot, the most tens scored on a hole, the shabbiest golf bag, the most lost balls, and the biggest lie told during the tournament.

In the inaugural year of the ITFDAGWDLGBWLTBFWA Open, Abe Lemmons, basketball coach for Oklahoma City University, set the local record for the shortest tee shot. He popped up his drive into a stiff wind and watched the ball land 15 yards behind him. For this dubious achievement he won a giant-sized jar of Geritol.

When Philadelphia Eagles head coach Buddy Ryan was an assistant coach for the New York Jets, he played in the 1969 ITFDAGWDLGBWLTBFWA Open and walked away with the best lie. He said that on the eighth hole his tee shot wedged itself in a tree. However, when no one was looking, the ball mysteriously fell right in the middle of the fairway. And even more remarkably, the words "good shot" had been penciled on the ball.

In 1970 a local duffer named Mike Perrett won the title of "Grand Chump" with a record-setting performance. Interestingly, another major title was won on the same day hundreds of miles away when Tony Jacklin captured the U.S. Open. Both golfers were right-handed, but the similarities ended there. Perrett shot 140; Jacklin 70. In smashing the previous ITFDAGWDLGBWLTBFWA Open mark of 125, Perrett lost three balls on the first hole and four on the fifth.

Prather Brown, who presented the "Grand Chump" award to Perrett, declared, "Some tournaments are of the highest rank. But this is about the rankest. The entry fee is indicative of the caliber of this tournament." The entry fee was $5.

"We would have had a bigger field," said tournament chairman Dave Story, "if we had made the fee $4.98."

DISQUIETING
DISQUALIFICATIONS

Championships have been lost, careers have been dashed, and hearts have been broken by unwittingly breaking a rule. Amazingly, these infractions aren't even committed on the course, yet they result in the ultimate punishment—disqualification. For "The Most Shocking DQ's in Tournament Play," The Golf Hall of SHAME inducts the following:

Jackie Pung
1957 U.S. Women's Open

Jackie Pung triumphantly walked off the 18th green of the Winged Foot Golf Club with a 72-hole score of 298, the apparent winner of the 1957 U.S. Women's Open.

It was the greatest moment in the golfing life of the jovial 235-pound Hawaiian-born housewife. Friends smothered her with embraces. Reporters peppered her with questions. The elated winner tried to be an accommodating champion as tears streamed down her round face.

But moments later those tears of joy turned into a cascade of anguish.

While fans hailed her as the new Women's Open queen, Jackie received heart-wrenching news—she was disqualified for signing an erroneous scorecard. The title—and the $1,800 first prize—instead would go to

Betsy Rawls, who had the second-best score of 299. Jackie burst into sobs.

It had been discovered that Betty Jameson, Jackie's playing companion and marker on the final round, had written a 5 for the fourth hole when, in fact, Jackie had scored a 6. However, the 18-hole total on the scorecard that Jackie signed was correct. In her haste and enthusiasm, Jackie didn't notice the mistake. All she saw was that her total score was accurate and she signed her card.

But the rigid and inflexible rules of golf were clear: If a competitor turns in a score for any hole lower than actually played, she shall be disqualified. So tournament officials had no choice but to DQ Jackie.

Ironically, Betty Jameson was disqualified at the same time for the identical reason. Jackie, who was Betty's marker, had mistakenly put down a 5 on Betty's scorecard on the same fourth hole after Betty had shot a 6. The only difference in the penalty was the consequence—Betty was not in contention, having shot an 85 in the final round.

The awards ceremony was almost too much for Jackie to bear. As the trophy was handed to Betsy Rawls, a few feet away a shattered Jackie (sitting in bottom left-hand corner of photo above) stared in stunned anguish.

"It was an awful mistake," admitted Jackie, her eyes red and her voice hoarse from crying. "It is due a great deal to the excitement. Both Betty and I knew we had 6's. My mistake and Betty's was in not repeating to each other what we had at that hole and seeing it was on the card.

"I was heartbroken. I thought I won this tournament. It meant a lot to me and my family. I would've won $1,800 and a bonus from the manufacturing company I represent. Now I have absolutely nothing to show for playing here this week."

Members of the Winged Foot Golf Club in Mamaroneck, New York, felt so sorry for Jackie that they raised $3,000 to help atone for her loss

142

of the first-place prize money. But the salve never quite soothed the wound.

Jackie, who would have made history by winning the U.S. Women's Open, saw her career fade into near oblivion.

Doug Sanders

1966 Pensacola Open

Moments after shooting a blistering 67 to take a four-stroke lead at the 1966 Pensacola Open, Doug Sanders signed dozens of autographs for his fans. He wrote his moniker on programs, note paper, and photos. In fact, he signed just about everything except the one thing that mattered most—his scorecard.

As a result, tournament officials had no choice but to hand Sanders the ultimate penalty—disqualification.

It was a punishment that a bitter Sanders, who was then the defending champion, claimed cost him $25,000 in winnings.

Just weeks earlier the PGA had sent tournament players a special bulletin reminding them that failure to check their scores and sign their scorecards could lead to a disqualification. Sanders was well aware of the rules. But because of his carelessness and some mitigating circumstances, a day of triumph turned to turmoil.

Sanders, winner of 20 PGA Tour events, played the back nine first during the second round at the Pensacola Country Club. When he holed out his final putt, there was no usual scorer's tent where he could go, sit down, review his round, and sign his card. The scorer's tent was at the 18th hole.

Sanders—a crowd favorite because he was from nearby Georgia and had attended the University of Florida—stepped off the course and into a crowd of cheering fans. "People swarmed all around me, asking for autographs," Sanders recalled. "I didn't want to push them off. I wanted to be nice. I must have signed my name a hundred times.

"I remember checking my card thoroughly three times and signing [playing partner] Johnny Pott's card, the one I kept. In all the confusion, I thought I signed my card. Then an official took my card to the scorer's table."

GOLF MAGAZINE

Sanders, who always made great copy, then went to the press room to hold court. "I had it wheeling and dealing out there today," he told reporters. While a smiling Sanders was answering reporters' questions with witty one-liners, PGA tournament supervisor Jack Tuthill whispered something in Sanders's ear. Sanders turned pale and grim and rushed out of the press room. Moments later Tuthill returned to drop a bombshell announcement—Sanders had been disqualified for failing to sign his scorecard.

"I'll admit I made a mistake in not signing the card," Sanders said. "But I think if I could show this consideration [signing autographs] to all the fans who were swarming around me, the same consideration [by PGA officials] could have been shown to me. I think it was a hasty decision. It was the most ridiculous thing I ever heard of. Imagine, I signed hundreds of autographs but I didn't sign my own card."

Tuthill defended the disqualification, stating that Sanders had violated Rule 38–2 in *The Rules of Golf*. "It's in the book," declared Tuthill. "We must enforce it. Furthermore, all the players had been warned less than a month before of the consequences."

Gay Brewer, who won the tourney after Sanders was DQ'ed, didn't shed any tears for his fallen rival. "I don't have any sympathy for Doug," Brewer told reporters. "He's always fooling around, being a good guy, signing autographs and so forth instead of taking care of his job." One pundit wrote that Brewer won the title on penmanship.

The next week, at the Doral Open, Sanders proved he had learned his lesson. He signed his name on the scorecard so big that no one could miss it.

Craig Stadler

1987 Andy Williams Open

Craig Stadler saved himself a $5 laundry bill . . . but it cost him a DQ and over $37,000.

"It was not an easy lesson to take, but life goes on," said the 1982 Masters champion. The Walrus was talking about his stunning woes caused by a towel he innocently used during the 1987 Andy Williams Open at Torrey Pines Golf Course in La Jolla, California.

On the 14th hole in the third round, Stadler's ball landed beneath a pine tree in a muddy lie. The only way to play the shot was from an awkward kneeling position. "I had one thought in mind," he said later. "It was muddy and damp out there, and I had on light-colored trousers." So he placed a towel on the wet ground, kneeled on it, and made his shot. Stadler didn't think anything more about it and finished the day among the leaders.

Stadler's nifty towel trick was replayed the next day by NBC, which

was broadcasting the final round. Immediately, astute golf fans lit up the tournament switchboard, claiming that Stadler had violated Rule 13–3 by illegally building a stance. Once they were alerted, PGA officials studied *Decisions on the Rules of Golf* by the USGA and the Royal and Ancient Golf Club of St. Andrews. There was no doubt that the use of a towel constituted an illegal improvement of one's stance and called for a two-stroke penalty.

Stadler—feeling pleased with himself for shooting a 270, good for second place—was strolling off the final green and calculating the amount of money he'd won when PGA Tour official Glenn Tait approached him with the bad news.

When Tait told him of the infraction, Stadler accepted the ruling and figured that the two-stroke penalty would drop him a notch or two in the tournament standings and cost him a few thousand dollars in winnings. Then Tait told him the really bad news.

Since Stadler hadn't realized he had broken any rule at the time he used the towel, he hadn't penalized himself the two strokes. Consequently, he'd turned in an incorrect scorecard—an infraction that calls for disqualification.

Had he not been ousted, Stadler would have finished tied for second place behind winner George Burns and would have earned $37,333.33.

"I thought about protesting," said Stadler. "The rule-book definition of a stance refers to a player placing his feet, and my feet weren't on the towel, but the situation seemed hopeless. Neither of my playing partners said anything about it at the time. There must have been a hundred people standing around the tree and nobody said anything. It's unfortunate. If somebody knew it [the rule], I wish they would have said something.

"I didn't read the decisions last year and I didn't read the rule book this year. One of these days I'm going to take a month off and read them both."

Seve Ballesteros

1980 U.S. Open

As Seve Ballesteros—Spain's most popular golfer—was flying from Madrid to the United States for the 1980 U.S. Open, he was struck by a dark premonition. "Seve," said a voice in his head, "you should not be going to the U.S. Open. Something bad is going to happen."

His premonition was right. Something bad did happen. The Spaniard missed his second-round tee off because he carelessly thought his starting time was an hour later. To his everlasting dismay, Seve had flown thousands of miles only to face the most talked-about disqualification of the decade.

The DQ stunned the golfing world because Ballesteros was considered one of the tournament favorites. At the age of twenty-three he reigned as the British Open and U.S. Masters champion.

Yet from the moment he arrived at Baltusrol Golf Club in Springfield, New Jersey, Ballesteros seemed doomed. He caught a bad cold, he was hurting from a chronically bad back, and he felt weak. In the first round he played poorly, missing fairways and blowing putts as he staggered to a five-over-par 75.

Then came that fateful morning of the second round. Believing that his tee time was 10:45 A.M., Seve and his brother Baldomero, who acted as his caddie, left their hotel at 9:25 A.M. for a two-mile ride to the golf course in a chauffeured car provided by tournament officials.

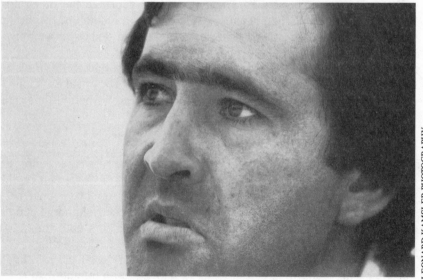

LEONARD KAMSLER PHOTOGRAPHY

The brothers joked the whole way and made no comments about the heavy traffic that clogged the streets and turned a normally five-minute drive into a 25-minute ride. They weren't aware that tee off was 9:45 A.M. Meanwhile, back at the first tee, his playing partners, Mark O'Meara and Hale Irwin, wondered what had happened to Ballesteros. As a courtesy to the Spaniard, they stalled as long as they could before hitting their tee shots.

When Seve finally arrived, a British journalist shouted, "Seve, you're late! You're overdue on the tee!" Ballesteros sprinted to the locker room, quickly pulled on his spikes, and rushed to the first tee. But it was too late—by seven minutes. In the distance Ballesteros could see O'Meara and Irwin putting on the green.

Following *The Rules of Golf*, starter John Laupheimer was forced to disqualify Ballesteros. The Spaniard exploded in fury, shouting that the penalty was too severe. "I'll never play in America again!" he thundered. (It was a threat he soon forgot.) Fuming mad, he returned to his hotel and flew back to Madrid that same evening.

It was fitting that this all happened on Friday the 13th.

Porky Oliver

1940 U.S. Open

Porky Oliver played the final round of the 1940 U.S. Open as an early bird and wound up a turkey.

In one of the most infamous infractions in U.S. Open history, Porky was disqualified because he teed off *too soon*. What made his premature start so devastating was that he finished tied for the championship. But because of his DQ, he wasn't allowed to compete in the playoff.

On the final day of the Open at Canterbury Golf Club in Cleveland, the short and squat, happy-go-lucky veteran touring pro was on top of his game. Playing with Dutch Harrison and Johnny Bulla, Porky was among the leaders after the first of two 18-hole rounds to be played that day.

Porky had just polished off a big noontime feast with Harrison in the clubhouse dining room when Bulla came in and told them a storm was brewing. Porky, claiming his "hammers were hot" (translation: his clubs were performing great), feared an afternoon washout would cool off his game. So he and his playing partners agreed to tee off early for the final round in the hopes of beating the storm.

Moments later, an assistant who had been guarding the box of official scorecards at the first tee rushed over to the starter, USGA official Joe Dey, who was eating lunch. Dey was told that Porky, Harrison, and Bulla had taken their cards from the box and were starting their final round.

Dey looked at the tee times and realized the threesome was teeing off twenty-eight minutes *before* they were officially scheduled. Dey raced out to the tee to stop them, but they had already hit their drives. When he caught up with them on the fairway, he informed them that they were playing without authority. Then he returned to the clubhouse to discuss the issue with the other officials.

Meanwhile, the threesome continued to play. However, Porky was so upset that he three-putted the first hole. But then he settled down to shoot a 69 for a 72-hole total of 287. That would have been good enough to tie Lawson Little and Gene Sarazen for the lead.

Back at the clubhouse, Porky was crushed to learn that he, Harrison, Bulla, and another threesome were disqualified for starting early. It didn't matter too much to the others because they weren't in contention. But to Porky it meant that he would not be in the championship playoff.

"Porky was pretty sore when he found out that he had been disqualified," recalled Harrison. "I don't blame him. But he took it like a man."

Actually, Harrison added, there was a silver lining to this calamity. "Before the incident, Porky wasn't well known. But afterwards, everyone had heard of Porky Oliver."

Fred Rowland

1988 British Amateur Championship

After spending months of practice and raising thousands of dollars, Kansas City golfer Fred Rowland eagerly flew 4,500 miles to Wales to play in the 1988 British Amateur.

But on the day of the biggest tournament of his life, he was disqualified for missing his start—because he was still in the bathroom when he was called to the first tee.

Months earlier, Rowland, a forty-nine-year-old insurance executive, was beaming with pride after being invited to play in the tourney by virtue of his performance at the U.S. Mid-Amateur Championship. To get ready for the British Amateur, he practiced evenings and weekends at Wolf Creek Golf Links, where he was six-time club champion. He hit balls in wind and rain to prepare for the bad weather over there. He even skipped local qualifying for the U.S. Open because he didn't want to tire himself out and lose a good day of practice.

When Rowland flew to Porthcawl, Wales, for the British Amateur, he felt on top of his game. On the big day he was ready; he was psyched. As expected, the weather was miserable, with rain driven by thirty-mile-an-hour winds.

After standing in the rain for an hour waiting to tee off, Rowland, holding an umbrella blown inside out, heeded nature's call. He ran over to a portable john about a hundred yards away. Because he had to take off his rain suit and then put it back on, he spent a little longer than expected. When he came toddling back to the tee, he saw one of his playing partners teeing off. Rowland was waiting to hit next.

But the head official, Sir Michael Reese, informed him, "Mr. Rowland, you weren't here when we called your name."

"Well, I was in the bathroom and my group is still on the tee," Rowland explained. Figuring that he might be slapped with a minor penalty for being a minute late, he asked, "What is it? A two-stroke penalty?"

"I'm afraid it's much worse than that," snorted Reese. "The penalty is disqualification."

The words bowled Rowland over like a sucker punch to the belly. His knees weakened and he thought for a moment that he was going to faint. "Gosh, I came a long way, not only from the U.S., but the *middle* of the U.S.," he pleaded. "Gosh, give me thirty lashes or something."

"Because you are an American, we gave you every consideration," said the unyielding Reese. "We called your name *twice* instead of once." He made it sound like a big deal. But to Rowland it was no bigger a deal than a philanthropist giving away free ice in the winter.

Reflecting later on his bad timing, Rowland said, "People say, 'Why didn't you slug him?' I immediately realized it was a lost cause. There was no reason making an ugly American scene out of it.

"I was wrong, that's all. I should have stayed there. What's really upsetting was that I didn't really have to go to the bathroom that badly."

Disqualifying Rounds

Pencil Whipped
David Eisner knocked his playing partners out of the 1971 U.S. Publinx Championship in two strokes—of a pencil.

In the opening round of the amateur tourney, he gave Larry Castagnoli a stroke less than he really shot on one hole. When Castagnoli carelessly signed the erroneous scorecard, he was disqualified.

The next day Eisner marked down another wrong score on a hole for Fred Lufkin, a former Publinx runner-up. Lufkin also failed to note the error before signing and was deked, too.

"If the tournament lasts long enough," said one player, "Eisner will win easy." But his golf clubs were no match for his pencil—he missed the cut by seven strokes.

Lost in the Shuffle
Lee Trevino was the unwitting victim of golf's version of three-card monte.

After the first round of the 1981 PGA Championship, Trevino and his playing partners, Tom Weiskopf and Lanny Wadkins, were checking their scorecards and passing them back and forth to sign. Trevino's scorecard was signed by his marker, Wadkins. But somehow in the shuffle, Weiskopf put his signature on Trevino's card where Trevino should have signed his name. Recalled Super Mex, "I got my card, checked it, saw two signatures, and turned it in." But because Trevino hadn't signed his own scorecard, he was disqualified.

One of Those Days

Touring pro John McMullin was disqualified not once but twice in the first round of the 1960 Motor City Open.

On the seventh hole, McMullin hit his second shot into a trap. Without thinking, he took a practice swing there. When he realized his mistake, he assessed himself a one-stroke penalty for taking a practice swing in a hazard. On the 13th hole, his second shot struck his caddie, costing him two more penalty strokes. On the 14th, he accidentally hit his ball while it was still moving, and assessed himself another penalty stroke.

Later, after signing his card, McMullin discovered that his penalty in the sand trap should have been two strokes, not one. So he was disqualified for signing an incorrect scorecard. Then he learned that he should have given himself two penalty strokes for hitting a moving ball on the 14th hole. So he was DQ'ed on that count, too.

"Two disqualifications and six penalty strokes," he said later. "I guess it's time to take a break." With that, he flew home to California and sat out the next six weeks to regain his composure.

BUNKER HELL

Hitting into a hazard is like going into debt—once you're in there, it's hell to pay getting out. Some golfers spend so much time in the sand, they're mistaken for Lawrence of Arabia. Others spend more time in the water than the HMS Queen Elizabeth. *For "The Most Hilarious Battles Ever Lost to a Hazard," The Golf Hall of SHAME inducts the following:*

Tom Weiskopf
1980 Masters Tournament

The 12th hole at Augusta National is called the "Golden Bell." And it has rung the death knell for the hopes of many golfers. But for whom did the bell toll most loudly? It tolled for thee, Tom Weiskopf.

He logged the most strokes over par—a whopping ten over—for a single hole in Masters history. And he did it by plunking five straight balls into the drink for a horrendous 13.

The Weiskopf calamity erupted on the bucolic 155-yard par-3 12th hole, which is fronted by Rae's Creek. It looks like heaven but it plays like Hell. Fuzzy Zoeller called it "the spookiest par-3 in golf," and 1940 Masters runner-up Lloyd Mangrum labeled it "the meanest little hole in the world."

Those are understatements to Weiskopf, winner of fifteen PGA Tour events and four-time Masters runner-up. When he reached the 12th during the first round of the 1980 Masters, he should have traded in his irons for a snorkel, mask, and fins.

Weiskopf, one of the year's top money winners, chose a seven-iron for his tee shot. The ball cleared the creek but trickled maddeningly back down a slope and into the water. After a penalty stroke, he hit a sand wedge from the drop area. The ball cleared the creek, only to spin back into the water just like the first shot did.

Weiskopf, known for his flawless swing, stood ramrod straight for several seconds, and then, with a stone face, extended his right arm. His caddie silently put another ball into his outstretched hand. Once again Weiskopf dropped, and once again he swung for the green, and once again his ball plopped into the creek. To the stunned amazement of the gallery and his fellow golfers, Weiskopf found himself locked in some diabolical groove: hit . . . splash . . . drop . . . hit . . . splash . . . drop . . .

After landing five straight balls in the water, Weiskopf, still valiantly hiding any emotion, had used up ten strokes. Finally, mercifully, his eleventh shot reached the fringe of the green, and from there he two-putted. Throughout this debacle, not once did Weiskopf flinch. Instead, he just walked off the green with his history-making 13.

"If you think I was composed, you're badly mistaken," he said later. "I was afraid to move my lips in front of the TV cameras. The commissioner probably would have fined me for what I was thinking.

"It was extremely embarrassing. The last time I got a 13 probably was when I was about fourteen years old.

"The thing was, I was trying to get over the water but couldn't. It got so absurd, it was funny. I had to laugh to myself. But if that had happened earlier in my career, I'd probably have jumped into the water with all those balls."

But Weiskopf's nightmare wasn't quite over. The next day, at the 12th, he once again hit his tee shot into the water. But this time he didn't take a drop. Instead he switched clubs, teed off again—and plunked another into the creek. Not wanting to be known forevermore as golf's greatest dowser, he finally reached the green with his third tee shot and finished the hole with a woeful seven. Unbelievably, on consecutive days Tom Weiskopf—a four-time Masters runner-up—had played the 12th in 14 over par.

"After that I got a lot of sympathetic letters," he recalled. "A few fans even sent me floating golf balls."

Hermann Tissies

1950 British Open

Flailing away in the bunkers like no other British Open competitor had ever done before, Hermann Tissies recorded the highest single-hole score in modern Open history—a bungling 15. What made this black mark even more inglorious was that he quadruple-triple-bogeyed the shortest hole on the course.

Tissies played, or rather misplayed, almost the entire hole from the sand traps, hopping back and forth from one to another to another. He spent so much time in the sand that his caddie got blisters from all the raking.

Tissies, a Hamburg amateur and Germany's most renowned golfer at the time, had traveled to the 1950 Open at Scotland's fabled Troon golf course to make a name for himself. That he did. He wound up starring in his own tragicomedy, "Bunker Hell." It was played out on the short 127-

yard par-3 eighth hole, noted for its tiny green known as the "Postage Stamp." Here was where Tissies got his worst licking ever.

It began when his tee shot (1) plopped into one of the three pot bunkers that guard the green. Tissies blasted out of the bunker (2), only to land in another. He pitched out (3), but shanked his next shot (4) back into a third bunker. From there he swung again (5) . . . and again (6) . . . and again (7) . . . and again (8). The ball refused to leave the sand. Finally, on his fifth shot from the same bunker he banged it out of the trap (9) . . . smack into the second bunker. Then he pitched the ball (10) right back into the first bunker.

Again, gripping his sand wedge with gritty determination—some of the grit coming from the sand blowing in his face—Tissies exploded out of the bunker (11) and onto the fringe of the green. The gallery didn't know whether to applaud because he had finally escaped the bunkers after all those shots or whether to remain silent for the very same reason.

By now Tissies was so wrecked that after chipping onto the green (12) he three-putted for his mortifying score of 15. It was the second worst single-hole tally ever in the entire history of the British Open. Only one golfer ever scored worse, and that happened in the very first Open way back in 1860, when a competitor, whose name has mercifully been lost or forgotten by the record keepers, took an atrocious 21 strokes on one hole.

Tissies, who finished the round with a deplorable 92, not only set the modern-day record, but instantly became the world's leading expert on pot bunkers.

The Scots, who take their golf as seriously as their plaids, were not amused. Echoing their feeling, *The Scotsman*, Scotland's newspaper of the day, called Tissies's disaster "a horrible species of Ping-Pong played between the bunkers."

Hans Merrell

1959 Bing Crosby National Pro-Am

Pro golf instructor Hans Merrell gave duffers a lesson in futility. Wallowing on the side of a vegetation-thick slope, he swatted and slugged his way to an atrocious 19—for one hole!

During the 1959 Bing Crosby National Pro-Am, Merrell set the inglorious Cypress Point record at the murderous, over-the-water, 222-yard par-3 16th hole. To reach the green, a golfer's drive must fly into the teeth of a prevailing wind and carry 200 yards across crashing waves, rocks, and a beach. The green rests on a 25-foot-steep hill that is covered with ice plant. This gremlin of the plant kingdom sports fleshy, four-inch spikelike leaves and gobbles up balls like a hungry Venus's-flytrap.

Merrell faded his drive and watched disconsolately as it fell onto the beach below the green. On his second shot he skulled the ball into the dreaded ice plant 20 feet away. Gingerly he walked into the vegetation and swung. The ball moved about a foot—into another ice plant. Then, with the form of a Mayan hacking through the jungle with a machete, Merrell wildly slashed at the ball five more times. The leaves went to tatters . . . and so did his score.

By now the ball had been buried so deep in the plant it was unplayable, so he picked it up, trudged back to the beach, and dropped the ball, taking a two-stroke penalty. Although his confidence was all but crushed, Merrell felt thankful that he was free from that cursed ice plant. But like a homing pigeon returning to its roost, his eleventh shot flew right back into the ice plant.

With his spirit fast draining away, Merrell took two more pokes. But each time, the ball fell backwards on the steep hill. Then he buried it again on his fourteenth shot . . . and with it, his sanity. He burst into uncontrollable laughter.

Proving he was a duffer but not a quitter, Merrell bravely marched back to the beach and dropped the ball for another two-stroke penalty. At last, on his seventeenth shot, he lofted the ball onto the green. From there he two-putted for an incredible 19. Merrell not only shattered the course record in botchery, but he also set a mark for the longest time ever taken to play a par-3 hole—32 minutes!

His playing partner, Bill Wehnes, an aircraft executive from Cleveland, was so awed by this historic moment that he asked Merrell for his ball so he could mount it as a trophy.

Ironically, in this best-ball tournament, Wehnes had sent two drives into the drink on the 16th and then quit the hole—because he figured that Merrell couldn't do any worse.

T. J. Moore

1978 Dryden Invitational

An innocent-looking water hazard turned T. J. Moore into a human divining rod. He found enough water to irrigate the Mojave Desert. The truth is, Moore won the hearts of duffers the world over—by pitching an astounding 20 straight balls into a pond!

Had he known what catastrophe awaited him, he could have played the hole in a submarine. It might have saved him the lasting shame of carding a mortifying 45 for one hole.

Water hazards have been known to play hellish games with a golfer's mind, but even the devil himself couldn't have screwed up a psyche with such infernal results. "It was a case where the harder you try, the worse

155

it gets,'' recalled Moore, a self-described weekend hacker. "It wasn't easy. I tell you what. You can *try* to put twenty balls in the water and you can't do it. Hell, I parred the hole the next day."

T.J. made his big splash, or rather splashes, during the 1978 Dryden Invitational at the Port Arthur Country Club in Texas. The forty-nine-year-old amateur was shooting "pretty good golf" in the first round until he reached the 381-yard par-4 18th hole, where a large pond guards the front of the green.

Hitting his third shot from 75 yards away, Moore plunked his ball into the water. He took a drop and tried again . . . and again . . . and again. Sickened by a helpless feeling in the pit of his stomach, T.J. found himself in a mental Twilight Zone, stuck in a groove from which he could not escape.

"By the fifth straight ball I felt like crawling in a hole," said Moore, an accountant in Port Arthur. "But my playing partners kept encouraging me, saying, 'You can do it.' But I was beginning to wonder. By the tenth shot in the water, I was ready to throw my clubs in the pond."

After number 12 took the plunge, T.J. had run out of balls and wanted to quit, but his fellow golfers talked him out of it. They were witnessing history—albeit shameful history—in the making. Besides, there was this perverse desire to see just how long, if ever, it would take for Moore to carry the pond. So they loaned him more balls. "They were behind me all the way," he said. "They wouldn't let me quit, or I would've done that much earlier. It was so aggravating."

Meanwhile, somebody alerted a local reporter who was covering the tournament and told him to rush over to the 18th hole. Word spread and people began crowding around the green much like rubberneckers passing a traffic accident.

Just when it looked like T.J. would wipe out the entire supply of balls from his playing partners, he hit his twenty-first wedge shot onto the green. The cheers from the gallery were as loud as those reserved for a hole in one. After two-putting, Moore walked sheepishly off the green and tallied up his 20 penalty strokes and marked down his whopping 45.

T.J., who after the tourney received the good sportsmanship award for doggedness, went straight from the water hole to the watering hole.

Sandra Haynie

1982 Henredon Classic

Sandra Haynie made a big splash in the 1982 Henredon Classic when she tangled with a water hazard. Her ball was high and dry but she sure wasn't.

Haynie, a member of the LPGA Hall of Fame and winner of 42 tournaments, was dueling with JoAnne Carner in an intense sudden-death playoff at Willow Creek Golf Course in High Point, North Carolina. At the 17th hole—the fifth hole of their playoff—Haynie's tee shot landed in a hazard area next to a lake on the left side of the fairway.

"When I was about to make my second shot, I was so tuned in to hitting it on the green that I didn't realize what was behind me," Haynie recalled. "I didn't realize that my heels were actually hanging on the edge of a bank where there was a five-foot drop into the water."

Haynie was already standing on the slope with the ball resting on higher ground. She needed to make a good shot because Carner was in perfect position for her approach.

Haynie took a healthy swing. The ball went one way but she went the other way. Her momentum carried her backwards and she toppled right into the water. "It was really a shock to me," she recalled. "It never occurred to me that this would happen. It was kind of like an auto accident. I was somewhat confused as to what had just happened. I was really discombobulated."

Said her caddie, Rick Aune: "It was so strange. Sandra hit the ball, I looked to see where it landed, and when I turned around, she was gone."

Haynie was helped out of the knee-high water by an official. With soaked pants, mud-splattered glasses, and a twisted ankle, Haynie calmly took off her shoes and poured the water out. Then she pulled off her socks and wrung them dry. Hurt and wet, she gamely played on, but her concentration had been shattered.

"My ball had fallen short of the green, and Joanne's second shot came within ten feet of the pin," said Haynie. "Now I was thinking about chipping close and making a four somehow. But I kind of wasn't in tune anymore." Haynie's third shot still came up short, and she two-putted for a bogey. Carner two-putted for par and the victory.

"After it was all over and I had time to think about it," said Haynie, "I thought it was pretty funny—and embarrassing." It was also costly. Haynie's unexpected dip in the water cost her $8,600—the difference between the checks for first and second place.

Roger Maltbie

1981 Tournament Players Championship

Roger Maltbie stormed a bunker with Rambo bravado . . . and staggered out with Jonah misery. He suffered more misadventures in the sand than a lost Libyan desert patrol.

In the final round of the 1981 Tournament Players Championship at Sawgrass in Ponte Vedra, Florida, Maltbie was playing sizzling golf and closing in on the leaders. But then on the long par-4 ninth hole, his second shot died in a stiff head wind. He needed another foot of carry but didn't get it as his ball buried under the lip of a bunker.

157

"It was one of those lies where you have to dig a big hole with your right foot to get a good stance," he recalled. "I mean, sand was up to my calf."

Rather than hit the ball sideways or backwards, Maltbie decided to blast the ball out of the bunker. With fierce determination he gripped his sand iron and took a tremendous hack. Like a scene out of *The Grapes of Wrath*, sand swirled in the wind and blew back in his face. Maltbie twisted his body and threw his arms over his face to shield his eyes. He protected himself from the sand, but not from the ball. It hit the lip of the bunker and rebounded into the back of his right arm, near his shoulder.

For being hit by his ball, Maltbie sustained a two-stroke penalty. But things only got worse. In trying to avoid the mini-sandstorm that he had created, Maltbie fell backwards into the bunker. When he stood up and wiped the sand off his face, he discovered that after the ball had hit him, it landed in one of his footprints. That meant he had to take an unplayable lie for another penalty stroke. Now he lay in six.

"I had to take my drop in the bunker, and wouldn't you know, the ball plugged!'' Maltbie said. "Then I bladed it across the green. I finally chipped on and two-putted for a smooth ten.

"I'm still trying to recover from that episode.''

Johnny Miller

1982 Memorial

It would make perfect sense if Johnny Miller wanted to alter the first two lines of Joyce Kilmer's classic poem to:

> *I think that I shall never see*
> *A hazard ugly as a tree.*

Setting an unofficial modern-day record, Miller hit the same tree not once, not twice, but three times on one hole.

"I don't often run up high scores, but a tree did get the better of me," said Miller, 1973 U.S. Open champion and 1974 PGA Player of the Year. His tree-mendous troubles came during the final round of the 1982 Memorial at Muirfield Village Golf Course in Dublin, Ohio.

Miller was in third place, one stroke off the lead on the 17th hole, when he smacked his drive into high rough. "I had an outside chance of winning if I could birdie the last two holes," he said. "I had to go for it." But in order to reach the green, Miller had to skirt a pine tree about 20 yards in front of him and directly in line with the flag.

"I hit my second shot right at the pine and it hit the top of the tree trunk and came straight back at me," he recalled. "I figured I couldn't possibly hit the tree again, so I aimed for the green and tried to get on."

To his shock and dismay, Miller's ball slammed into the same tree trunk again and rebounded toward him. "Now I was on a downslope in about 12 inches of rough. I was down in the hollow in front of the green, but still behind the tree.

"After I had hit it the second time, I told myself, 'Well, what are the odds of that? I'll never do that again.' So I tried to go to the left of the tree. But I hit it a third straight time—perfectly, dead center.

"At least the ball bounced clear of the tree. I hit my next shot on the green and two-putted for a triple-bogey seven. Then I came back to birdie 18. If I could have traded my seven on 17 for a birdie or even a par, I would have finished close to first."

A par on the 17th would have

given Miller a fifth-place tie and a check for $10,150. Instead he finished tied for twenty-second, worth $3,404.

"In all my years in golf, I've never seen anything like what happened to me on the 17th. Three times, dead center on the tree trunk. A lot of money went down the drain, I know that."

Bruce Devlin
1975 Andy Williams San Diego Open

Bruce Devlin has a water hazard named after him—for which he paid a hefty price both in money and in shame.

He earned the dishonor during the last round of the 1975 Andy Williams San Diego Open at Torrey Pines Golf Course. Devlin was two shots behind the leader going into the final hole, a par-5 guarded by a pond. "I felt I could win the tournament if I made a three on the final hole," he recalled. "I needed to eagle it."

The Australian-born golfer, winner of eight PGA Tour events, crushed his drive into the right rough, but still was in good position to reach the green in two. He whipped out his four-wood and let it rip. At first his spirits soared with the ball as it carried the pond in front of the green and hit the bank about 18 inches short of the fringe. But then the ball slowly and agonizingly trickled back down into the pond, coming to rest a few inches below the water.

Once he recovered from the jarring disappointment, Devlin knew he had two options. He could take a drop plus a penalty stroke or try to blast out of the water. "I had to go for it," he said. "I was sure I could hit it out with my wedge."

With hopes of an eagle dashed, Devlin needed a miracle shot for a birdie attempt. He swung at the ball, sending up a huge splash but not the ball. Now the best he could hope for was a par. So he swung again. This time the ball blooped onto the bank . . . and rolled back into the water.

"Even then I was not going to take a drop," he recalled. "I was going to play it until I got it on the green." It took him a lot longer than he expected. To his ever-growing shock, his next four shots from the water were just as bad as the previous ones. Each time, the ball feebly spurted out of the pond and onto the bank only to slip back into the water.

The gallery, not knowing whether to admire his determination or question his sanity, remained silent. Finally, on his ninth shot—his seventh attempt from the pond—Devlin blasted onto the green and holed out for a devastating ten.

"With each shot I kept thinking that the prize money I'd win was getting cheaper and cheaper," he recalled. "The first shot cost me a chance at $40,000. The second $20,000. The third one $8,000, and the fourth one $2,000."

Devlin's fortunes had sunk far lower than had his ball. From third place before his watery misadventure, he plunged all the way down to a tie for thirtieth worth $1,032.

Since such disasters don't happen every week on the PGA Tour, the management at Torrey Pines decided to commemorate this historically shameful moment by putting up a plaque and naming the water hazard after the Australian word for pond. It's now known fondly as "Devlin's Billabong."

Animal Hazards

It Ain't Hippo to Miss the Fairway

Paul Burley discovered that if you don't hit the fairway in South Africa, you could wind up running for your life.

During a 1987 tournament at the Hans Merensky Country Club in Phalaborwa, South Africa, Burley, of Grimsby, England, sliced his drive into the bushes guarding the right side of the third hole. As he was lining up his second shot, he heard a loud crash behind him.

"Suddenly, two monstrous hippos, one behind the other, came crashing out of the bush toward us," he recalled. "My caddie threw down my bag and was off across the fairway like a shot, and I was right on his tail. My playing partners and their caddies were ahead of us as we screamed and ran across the fairway and into the rough looking for a tree to get up.

"There weren't any big enough, so it was most fortunate when the two hippos suddenly veered off and went back the way we had just come. Then we all just sat down and had ourselves a good laugh."

A Mooing Experience

At the Borders Club in northern England, about 150 golf balls a week were being eaten by cows on the fairways, to the udder astonishment of golfers.

In 1967 the animals suddenly developed a taste for golf balls. Apparently alerted by the smell of humans, the cows ambled behind a wall guarding the blind third hole. Then, whenever they heard the thump of a ball hitting the fairway, the bovine closest to the ball moseyed out onto the course and lapped it up. By the time the golfer had reached the spot where the ball had landed, the ball had been digested. One player had four balls eaten in two holes.

Because the owner of the cows had legal grazing rights on part of the course, the club came up with a local rule: "If a player's golf ball is consumed by a cow during the course of play, the player is allowed to drop another ball adjacent to the spot, without penalty."

Where's the Beef?

For a time the 1984 St. Andrews Trophy Match looked more like the running of the bulls in Pamplona, Spain.

While playing on the 18th green at the Staunton Course on the Devon coast of England, four golfers suddenly found themselves in the midst of a thundering cattle stampede.

According to a news account, "The cattle, forty or fifty strong, came in a gallop round a sand hill, through the rough, and then took a sharp dogleg to the right up the 18th fairway towards the green and the clubhouse, where its occupants did a hasty double-take, wondering whether something extra had been slipped into their drinks.

"Grabbing the first weapon he could find, [tournament official] John Goodban laid his hands on a red flag, and with warlike cries from members of the Championship committee, they raised a fair old gallop themselves, getting to the green just in time to head the herd away."

Love Is Ducky

During first-round action of the 1972 Atlanta Classic, Dave Hill, Bert Yancey, and Brian Allin were gunning for birdies on the ninth hole when they were interrupted by a drake's dalliance with a duck.

As the golfers were studying their putts, the gallery erupted in applause. It took a while for the bewildered players to figure out the reason for the ovation. At the edge of the green, a duck and a drake had struck up a romance and were not the least bit shy in consummating their affair.

The applause turned to boos when marshals from the morals squad shooed the courting couple from the green. Despite the distraction, all three golfers got their birdies. So did the drake.

Land Snakes Alive!

During the 1972 Singapore Open Jimmy Stewart—the golfer, not the actor—was forced to play killer golf.

As Stewart approached the ball for his second shot on the third hole, a ten-foot-long cobra slithered toward it from the other side. Whipping out a three-iron, a frightened Stewart clubbed the serpent to death.

But just when Stewart breathed a sigh of relief, he was shocked once again. A smaller snake emerged from the mouth of the dead snake. He slew that one, too.

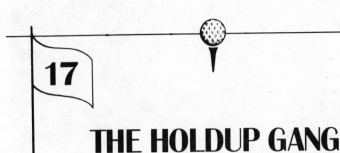

THE HOLDUP GANG

Nothing so irritates golfers as slow players. These turtles play as though each shot requires the care of a space-shuttle launch. They take more time reading a green than they do a James Michener novel. The slowpokes don't just check the grass; they study the roots. For "The Most Flagrant Cases of Slow Play," The Golf Hall of SHAME *inducts the following:*

Cyril Walker

1930 Los Angeles Open

Cyril Walker was the slowest player in pro golf—he made inchworms look like speed demons. Walker was so pokey he should have changed his name to Crawler.

His maddening dillydallying drove players and tournament officials nuts. The one time he moved fast was when police hustled him off the course at the 1930 Los Angeles Open after he was disqualified for slow play.

Walker, a slight 130-pound Englishman who won the 1924 U.S. Open, played the first round at the Riviera Country Club like he always did—as if he were strolling along the banks of the Avon, stopping to smell the flowers. What took his competitors three hours to play took him five hours.

In the second round, his tarrying became intolerable. Before each approach shot, Walker lived up to his name by leisurely walking the

hundred yards or so to the green and then sauntering back to his ball. Next, he felt the grass around the ball and picked up imaginary pebbles, leaves, and tiny pieces of cut grass. Then he took several practice swings with different clubs. Once he selected the right one, he took his stance, waggled the club at least a dozen times, and finally hit the ball.

Walker's dawdling created an enormous traffic jam for those playing behind him. The marshals tried to hurry him along, but he remained oblivious to their pleas. At the sixth hole, a tournament official warned him that if he didn't speed up, he'd be disqualified. Walker glared at the official and snarled, ''You won't disqualify me. I'm Cyril Walker, a former U.S. Open champion. I've come 5,000 miles to play in your diddy-bump tournament, and I'll play as slow as I damn well please.''

When he eventually arrived at the ninth hole—nearly an hour later than he should have—he was informed that he had been disqualified for slow play.

"The hell I am!" Walker snapped. "I came here to play, and I'm going to play!" He shoved the official aside and headed for the green to putt. The official, determined to stick to his guns, then summoned two burly policemen to escort Walker off the course. They asked him politely to leave, but the arrogant golfer just scoffed at them, believing they would never lay a hand on a former U.S. Open champion. He was wrong.

The two cops grabbed Walker by the elbows and carted him off as he kicked and screamed in protest. They dumped him at the clubhouse door and told him not to come back or he'd be swinging his clubs behind bars.

From then on most pros on the Tour refused to play with Walker or behind him. So accommodating tournament officials often let him play alone with only his caddie and scorer by his side. And there was one other concession. They always sent Walker off last.

Don January
1963 Phoenix Open

Never has a pro golfer waited as long as Don January did, hoping for a putt to drop. With his ball teetering on the lip of the cup, January waited an astounding *seven* minutes for the leaner to fall. But it never did.

"The ball stayed there for seven minutes, but it felt like seven years," declared playing partner Gary Player, who was the player most peeved over the irritating waiting game.

Seemingly taking as long as his surname, January set the unofficial record for tarrying on a green. He did it during the final round of the 1963 Phoenix Open at the Arizona Country Club after he, Player, and Johnny Pott had reached the 18th green. While Pott and January were no longer in contention, Player needed to make a crucial four-foot putt to tie for the lead and force a playoff. But before Player could putt, he had to watch January, who was five shots back, try to knock in a ten-footer for fifth place.

"It was late in the day and the wind was blowing and howling," recalled January, winner of 12 Tour events. "I putted first and the ball stopped right on the lip, half in and half out. I walked up to it and looked at it very carefully. Hell, the ball was moving, and there's a rule that says you can't hit a ball that's moving. It's a penalty if you do hit it. I called Johnny over and he said, 'It's moving.' I called Gary over and he said, 'It's moving.' "

Measuring devices at MIT couldn't have been any more precise than the eyes of this threesome. If the ball moved a mere quarter of an inch in seven minutes, its rate of speed would have been about .0000338 miles per hour. That's 338 ten millionths of a mile per hour, give or take a ten millionth.

"So we waited and waited," said January. It wasn't as if his putt was for a championship or big money. January was shooting for an extra $250, the difference between fifth and seventh place. "We must have waited five minutes. [No, Don, according to eyewitnesses, it was definitely seven minutes.] Finally, I had to tap it in."

Player, who was obviously anxious to putt, had been getting madder by the minute. By the seven-minute mark his blood had reached the boiling point. If January hadn't tapped in the ball, Player was ready to knock it in for him. "January didn't have a right to wait for seven minutes for that putt to drop," recalled Player. "It wasn't ever going to drop, not without hitting it.

"It was very nerve-wracking for me, especially knowing that I needed a birdie to tie Arnold Palmer for the lead." When it was finally his turn to putt, Player, still irked by all that waiting, missed his four-footer and blew his chance to tie. He finished one stroke behind winner Arnold Palmer.

Although Player was ticked at January, he kept it to himself—for a while. "We signed our cards and nothing was said," recalled January. "I had a locker next to Gary's, and he didn't say anything to me there, either. The next day, though, the papers quoted him as saying that I cost him the tournament. He even called the commissioner [Joe Dey] to complain."

Today, Player has mellowed. "I'm not bitter," he said recently. "In those days, those sorts of things happened."

January said the incident did one good thing. "It changed the rule. Back then I was within my rights to wait that long. Now if a player waits longer than ten seconds, he is assessed a penalty stroke."

Not surprisingly, it's called "The January Rule."

Archie Compston

For sheer arrogance on the golf course, Archibald Edward Wones Compston had no peer.

Displaying a snobbishness never seen before or since in golf, Archie took his own sweet time on the links, without giving a damn about what the rest of the field thought.

As one of England's greatest golfing personalities in the 1920s and 1930s, Compston played with the deliberateness and haughtiness of royalty . . . and expected to be treated as such.

The tall, ruggedly handsome Compston was a good golfer, but not worthy of any lordship. He was the runner-up in the 1925 British Open and a Ryder Cup player in 1927, 1929, and 1931.

What set him apart from other golfers was the way he drove his playing

partners to distraction—he loitered after each shot, so that his every whim could be met by his caddies. He didn't have just one caddie. Or even two. Archie insisted on having *three* caddies by his side!

He found it much too déclassé to have only one caddie. "My dear man," he once explained to a reporter, "how do you possibly expect one lone soul to attend to all my needs?" Compston employed one caddie to tote his bag; another to carry his sweater, raincoat, and umbrella; and a third whose sole responsibility was to take care of Archie's smoking paraphernalia.

Aside from his slow, regal, leisurely gait on the fairway, Archie imperiously held up play because of the importance he attached to his smokes. He didn't just light up a cigarette while walking toward his ball. Oh no. He made a big production out of it.

Like a wine steward choosing a fine Bordeaux for a blue-blood gourmet, Compston's tobacco caddie had to choose the right kind of smoke for each hole. On short holes Archie would stop after his tee shot, loftily hold out his hand, and have a lighted cigarette placed between his fingers. Then, with his nose in the air, he'd take a few long drags before sauntering down the fairway.

On longer holes he required a thin Cuban stogie. Each puff off the cigar brought him to a standstill as he basked in its aroma. Whenever Archie reached a dogleg, he waited until the tobacco caddie prepared a special, hand-carved, curved-stemmed meerschaum pipe. Compston celebrated his birdies and eagles by eschewing his smokes. Instead, he carved off just a little piece of his Piper Heidsieck chewing tobacco.

The tobacco caddie had one other task—talk to the ball. Whenever Compston hit a bad hook or slice and shouted, "No! No!" it was the caddie's job to yell at the ball, "Get back! Get back!"

Most of the golfers playing either with Archie or behind him would have liked to have heard his caddie tell him, "Get going! Get going!"

Lady Golfers
1960 Bank of Montreal Tournament

Golf was never played more slowly or ridiculously than at the first annual Bank of Montreal women's tournament.

In 1960, female employees of the bank in Vancouver, British Columbia, made plans to hold their tourney at Gleneagles, a quaint nine-hole course in West Vancouver.

Club pro Ron Fitch marked off 90 minutes for the starting times of the 60-woman tournament. But when more than half the women showed up without clubs and had to rent them from him, Fitch realized it was going to be a long day. However, not in his wildest imagination could he foresee just how long a day it would be.

"As soon as they started teeing off, I could see there weren't two good golfers among them," Fitch recalled. The first foursome hacked and clubbed their balls as though they were beating snakes. Each member of the next group set a goal to break 40—for the hole. The following foursome could have used handicaps twice the number of their bra sizes.

Whenever a woman hit a ball that rolled ten yards, her playing partners would shout, "Great shot!" Fitch knew he had to do something to speed up play. So after each member of a foursome had hit five or six shots and finally moved at least 100 yards away from the tee, Fitch sent off the next group. He knew the ladies in the fairway were in no danger of being struck by a drive off the tee.

The women were so spread out over the first hole—and off it to either side—that Fitch figured it was now safe to send golfers off in groups of *eight*. Soon the entire first fairway and the surrounding rough, ditches, bunkers, and trees teemed with the biggest contingent of duffers ever seen on one hole.

By the time he dispatched the final eightsome, Fitch saw a sight he couldn't have dreamed in his scariest nightmare. There they were, five dozen blundering, giggling women flailing at balls, searching for balls, inflicting terrible wounds on balls, or missing balls altogether.

As one of Fitch's golfing buddies described it: "The scene is reminiscent of a ragged female army assaulting a beach on some foreign shore, except that the air is filled with shrieks of laughter." By now the first fairway was so pockmarked with divots it looked as if the course had been strafed in a bombing run.

At this shamefully slow rate there was a better than even chance that the women would have to bivouac for the night if they hoped to finish all nine holes. "I was ready to pull my hair out," said Fitch. No one would have blamed him if he had—especially after what happened next.

From the starter's shack Fitch could see the fifth hole, and he kept an eye out for the first group of golfers. But the fairway remained empty. Concern creased his brow as he checked his watch. Enough time had elapsed—even for these slowpokes—to at least be playing on the fifth hole. Then he noticed that the last few groups, who were still grappling with the first hole, had put down their clubs and were lying under the fir trees. No one in sight was moving.

Fearing an accident or a death, Fitch sent an assistant out to investigate. The assistant returned white-faced and gave a rambling account that Fitch refused to believe. He decided to check out the story for himself.

"I was dumbfounded by what I saw," Fitch recalled. "These women were having an honest-to-goodness picnic right on the third green! With food and drinks and everything! Apparently, when the first few groups arrived at the hole, they were all pretty tired. They had already taken enough strokes for a whole round. Well, they decided that the green was the perfect place for a picnic."

The women unzipped the pockets of their golf bags and pulled out blankets which they spread over the green. Then they brought out sandwiches, snacks, fruits, cheeses, wine, beer—and even flasks of gin and rum.

Fitch, who was in his first month as the club pro, walked up to the picnickers and politely but firmly told them that Gleneagles was not a picnic ground but a golf course and that they would have to either play golf or leave the course. Reluctantly, they complied.

"I thought that if this is what normally happens when you run a golf course, then I wouldn't last another week," said Fitch. "The last thing I said to them was, 'Glad you had fun, but, please, promise you won't come back.' "

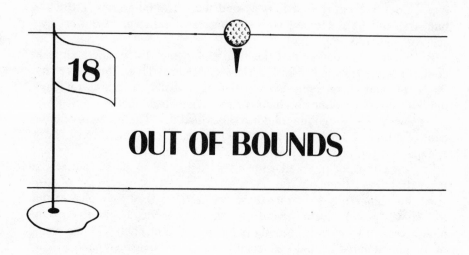

OUT OF BOUNDS

Off the course, pro golfers are supposed to spend part of their free time sharpening their skills on the practice range, the putting green, or even in their hotel rooms. But the skills they sharpen aren't necessarily for golf. For "The Most Foolish Behavior off the Course," The Golf Hall of SHAME inducts the following:

Walter Hagen and Joe Kirkwood
Tijuana, Mexico, 1928

In the wackiest match of their lives, the great Walter Hagen and his sidekick Joe Kirkwood turned the streets of Tijuana, Mexico, into their own fairways.

Kirkwood—an Australian-born trick-shot artist and tournament player who won the California, Houston, and Illinois Opens in 1923—was one of the Haig's best friends. Occasionally they took time out to play in golfing exhibitions throughout the world. One of Kirkwood's favorite tee shots was hitting off the back of an elephant in Africa and India (see photo).

In 1928 the pair played at Caliente Golf Course in Tijuana, where the fairways were nothing more than parched, arid ground. Afterwards, in the locker room, Kirkwood told Hagen, "It was like playing in a desert out there, with the dry heat and all that dust. Next time I'll bring a camel."

"You're just spoiled," kidded Hagen. "You just want to play on wide, manicured fairways and big smooth greens."

"I can play on any course," countered Kirkwood.

"Oh yeah?" said Hagen. "Tell you what. How about we make our own course and play on it?"

"What do you mean?"

"Let's use the streets of Tijuana. We'll play from the locker room back to our hotel room. The first one who gets back and knocks the ball into the toilet bowl wins."

"You're on. For how much?"

"Let's keep it friendly," said Hagen. "Fifty bucks."

Each with a caddie by his side, the pair set out from the clubhouse on the mile-long "course" to their hotel. As a growing crowd of golfing aficionados clustered around them making side bets, Hagen and Kirkwood banged their shots down the dusty driveway of the golf club and onto the main street.

Followed by a cheering gallery in sombreros and sandals, the pair played through the center of town. The zany twosome drove their balls past giggling, barefoot, tortilla-making muchachas and through an open-air fruit market of startled merchants. All the while, Hagen and Kirkwood dodged trucks, buses, and donkey-hauled carts, and more often than not brought traffic to a screeching halt.

Hagen arrived at the hotel grounds first, ahead of Kirkwood by about a minute. Walter lofted a shot that carried the flower beds. Then he belted the ball into the lobby and played it up the stairs, down the corridors, and finally into their room.

But infuriatingly, the Haig failed to knock his ball into the toilet bowl because he couldn't pick it off the tile floor. After a dozen unsuccessful attempts, he saw Kirkwood enter the bathroom. "Move over," said Joe. Then, with one deft swing of his pitching wedge, he plopped his ball into the toilet. Said Kirkwood, "Now that's what I call a fifty-dollar splash."

Jack Nicklaus and
John Montgomery Sr.
Lost Tree Village, Florida

Never in the history of golf has the birthday of a superstar like Jack Nicklaus been treated with such irreverence.

Like watching a chip shot that rims the cup, Nicklaus has groaned over some of the wacky gifts he's received from his good friend John Montgomery. During the 1980s John has left on Jack's front doorstep such presents as a braying donkey, a bleating goat, 200 squawking chickens, a stripteasing chimpanzee . . . and four tons of stinky horse manure! Nicklaus has taken it all in stride—except for the horse manure. That time he exacted a measure of revenge as powerful as the smell.

Montgomery—president of Executive Sports, a firm that manages about 40 big golf tournaments a year—has been a close friend of the Golden Bear since the early 1970s. That's rather remarkable considering all the birthday pranks he's pulled on Jack.

Before sunrise one morning on a Nicklaus birthday, Montgomery quietly pulled up at Jack's waterfront home in Lost Tree Village, an exclusive community in North Palm Beach, Florida. John's car was toting a trailer carrying a donkey. "We got the donkey in the driveway, but there was nowhere to tie him up, so we tied him to the sideview mirror of one of Jack's cars parked in front of the house," Montgomery recalled. "Then we tiptoed away. We got about a hundred yards away when the donkey began heehawing. We broke into a run, hopped into our car, and laughed the whole way back home [to nearby Delray Beach]."

Only later did John learn that the donkey, in trying to escape, broke off the rearview mirror and dented the car. It finally got loose and was found ambling in Lost Tree Village wearing a ribbon around its neck with a card that said "Happy Birthday, Jack."

Nicklaus, not wanting to give Montgomery the satisfaction of knowing the donkey prank worked, made the family promise to remain silent about the present. "John was trying everything he could to break us, but none of us did," recalled Jack. "Nobody said a word for six or seven weeks.

172

Then, after a party, he discovered that somebody had sideswiped his car. I couldn't help myself so I said, 'It must have been a hit-and-run donkey.' " Montgomery roared and knew for the first time that Nicklaus had received his donkey.

After that episode Nicklaus asked the guards at the Lost Tree gatehouse not to cooperate with Montgomery. So for Jack's next birthday John schemed to invade Nicklaus's home by water. "I knew the guard gate was impenetrable, so I borrowed a boat," Montgomery recalled. "A friend of mine gave me 200 chickens. We loaded them on the boat and took them to Jack's house in the middle of the night. I let some of them loose on his putting green, some on the grass tennis courts, some near the front entrance. Then I took a sack of bird feed and just threw it all over because I knew when chickens get scared, they flock together. They were all over the yard by daylight."

The chickens caused a peck of trouble for Nicklaus. Their excretions damaged the putting green, the tennis court, and tile in a new addition in the guest house. "Jack had to put a hundred new plugs in his putting green and tennis court and regrout the new floor," said Montgomery. "Also, when the chickens went for the feed, they left bill imprints all over the yard. Barbara [Nicklaus's wife] was going to kill me."

Then, for the crowning touch, Montgomery had a friend who was a policeman call the Nicklauses. "The cop said he had a complaint about chickens in the yard and wanted to know if we had permits or else get rid of them," recalled Jack.

"The funniest thing was a few weeks later when the lawn crew spotted some plants growing in the backyard. It was from the seed. One of the lawn men said, 'Mr. Nicklaus, there's marijuana growing in your yard.' "

But the all-time most shameful birthday gift that John ever gave Jack was a four-ton pile of horse manure. "A truck dumped a stack ten feet high in front of his door," Montgomery said proudly. "I had no idea it would be that high. On the pile was a sign saying 'Happy Birthday, Jack.' But then it backfired . . ."

That night Nicklaus got his revenge. By the time the guests, including John and his wife Nancy, arrived at Jack's for his birthday party, the horse manure had been hauled away except for several garbage bags full of the stuff. Nicklaus, knowing that Montgomery never locked his car, told Barbara that he was going to fill John's car with the manure. "Barbara just wanted me to put the bags in his car," Jack recalled. "But I told her, 'It wasn't delivered in bags, so it's going in his car without bags.' "

Recalled Montgomery, "We got ready to leave, and when I opened the side door to let Nancy in, the manure started falling out. Jack had somebody stack it up in the backseat of Nancy's Eldorado. She'd just had the leather seats of her car cleaned, and boy was she mad.

"We tried to get most of it out. As we were driving home, Nancy said,

'My door's not closed all the way.' So she opened the door and the wind swirled in and blew dried pieces of manure in her hair and all over her dress.

"I kept laughing, but she wanted to kill me. I told Jack later he didn't get me back by piling the horse manure in Nancy's car. He got back at me because I had to ride forty-five minutes home and listen to my wife harangue me for all the dirty deeds I've pulled on him."

Roger Maltbie

1975 Pleasant Valley Classic

In the zaniest quandary ever experienced by a tournament winner, Roger Maltbie lost, within hours, the very thing he'd worked so hard to earn—the $40,000 first-prize check.

Maltbie, then a rookie on the PGA Tour, was delirious with joy after winning the 1975 Pleasant Valley Classic, the biggest payoff in his life up to then. Usually when a pro wins a tournament, he is handed a large dummy check made out of cardboard. But this time Maltbie received a real check. It was much easier to handle than the oversized check, but also much easier to lose, as he soon discovered.

The Malt-man, who has always partied with the same vigor as he has golfed, stuffed the winner's check in his pocket, which was already bulging with an additional $600 in cash. Feeling happy and rich, Maltbie chose to celebrate his good fortune at a bar called T.O. Flynn's in Worcester, Massachusetts. "When I got there," Maltbie recalled, "I pulled out the cash, threw it on the bar, and told everybody to get drunk on me and have fun."

Maltbie, of course, took himself up on his own words, quaffed a few too many, and closed the place up. The next morning he suffered a dilemma worse than any hangover. "When I woke up the first thing I wanted to do was buy a paper to read about what a hero I was," recalled Maltbie, the eighth-leading money winner in 1985. "I reached in my pants pocket for some money. No cash. No check, either.

"I sat down on the bed for a half hour and tried to reconstruct what had happened the night before. I just sat there trying to figure out what the hell happened, where did I go. Finally, I remembered—T.O. Flynn's!"

Hoping against hope that some honest soul had found the lost check, Maltbie called the bar, only to learn that the cleanup crew hadn't turned in any such check. Fighting hard to quash a panicky feeling in the pit of his stomach, Maltbie phoned Cuz Mingolla, the general chairman of the tournament, and with great embarrassment told his tale of woe. Mingolla said he'd stop payment on the check and cut Maltbie a new one.

Minutes later Maltbie received a call from Flynn's. The lost check had been found by a cleaning lady. She had been vacuuming the floor when she noticed a piece of paper that was all crumpled up in a ball and wouldn't go through the vacuum hose. She picked it up and was stunned to see it was a check for $40,000. She promptly turned it in.

Before the check was returned to tournament officials, a photocopy was made. The photocopy was framed and hanged over the bar at Flynn's, which is now closed.

Maltbie was given a replacement check. The original rumpled check is in the possession of Ted Mingolla, who took over for his late father Cuz. "We'll nail the check to the [tournament office] wall so it doesn't get lost again," said Ted.

And what happened to Maltbie's $600? "That," said the Malt-man, "was all drunk up."

Toney Penna
1938 Biltmore Open

In one of the all-time great pranks, three golfers left fellow competitor Toney Penna totally em-bare-assed.

During the 1938 Biltmore Open in Miami, Penna and Jimmy Demaret shared a hotel room that had a connecting door to a room shared by Willie Goggin and Tommy LoPresti.

One day, after the practice round, Demaret, Goggin, and LoPresti decided to pull a practical joke on Penna that has become legend on the PGA Tour.

Penna had just taken a bath when he heard a knock on the door. Wrapping a towel around him, Penna cautiously opened the door and peered out to see Demaret. "Why don't you just come in?" Penna asked.

No sooner were the words said than LoPresti, who had sneaked up behind Penna by coming through the connecting door, snatched his towel. Then he pushed Penna out into the hall, slammed the door, and locked it. Meanwhile, Demaret dashed into the adjoining room and bolted the door. Penna was left stark naked in the hall in front of the elevators.

Frantically looking for a place to hide, Penna made a beeline for a mop closet. He crouched inside, but despite his small stature, he still couldn't completely conceal himself because the closet wasn't big enough.

Just then three women emerged from the elevator and walked down the hall in his direction. Unable to squeeze himself any farther into the tiny closet, he held the mop strategically between his legs and hoped they wouldn't notice. Having never seen a naked man hiding behind a mop, the women stared at him in wide-eyed amazement. Trying to salvage a wee bit of decorum in this otherwise mortifying situation, Penna said, "Good afternoon, ladies."

After the women scurried down the hall giggling loudly, he dashed to the door of his room and beat on it with the mop handle. He could hear the three perpetrators inside howling with laughter. But this wasn't funny to Penna. "Open up the door or I'm gonna bust it down!" he shouted.

But to his chagrin the doors to the elevator opened again, so he made a hurried retreat to the mop closet. When Penna noticed it was a man, he said to him, "Hey, Mac, do me a favor and call the house detective." The startled man looked at Penna as if he were a lunatic. "I'm not nuts," Penna told him. "Those idiots I'm rooming with have locked me out of the room and I can't get back in."

"Okay," said the man. "I'll send the cavalry right away."

A few minutes later the house detective arrived and opened the door to Penna's room—and not a moment too soon, because a group of women was emerging from the elevator.

"I almost went through him [the house detective] getting into my room," recalled Penna. "The three others were still howling in the other room. They had been smart enough to lock the connecting door, or all three of them might have had their obituaries written that afternoon."

Janice Irby

Casselton, North Dakota, 1987

Janice Irby now knows that explosion shots are for bunkers, not ovens. And she now knows that when baking a cake, you do *not* put golf balls inside.

In 1987, when her husband John was about to turn 30, he told her that he didn't want anyone to know about his birthday. But Janice had other ideas. Since she and her husband are both avid golfers, she decided that for his thirtieth birthday she would bake him a chocolate sheet cake decorated in a golfing theme. Then she would invite some friends over to the couple's golf-course home in Casselton for a surprise party.

Just before popping the cake into the oven, Janice had another brainstorm. "I thought as a joke it would be great to put some golf balls in the cake," she recalled. "So I dropped four new ones in the batter and put the whole thing in the oven.

"About ten minutes before I was supposed to take the cake out, the golf balls exploded. The jackets remained fairly intact and so did the cores. But rubber filaments were hanging all over the oven coils. Luckily, the oven itself wasn't damaged. But the house smelled of burning rubber.

"My cake looked as if someone took a shotgun and plugged a couple of rounds into it. But otherwise it was intact and seemed quite edible. So I went ahead and decorated the cake with icing to look like a fairway, and I turned the holes into water hazards and bunkers."

When her husband came home, he asked what that horrible smell was. Janice told John there was a problem with the oven and then hustled him out to dinner. When they returned home, John was greeted with the surprise party.

"We ate the cake," she said. "I just made sure everybody ate around the holes. When John found out about the exploding golf balls, he was definitely embarrassed about how stupid I was. It just never occurred to me that those balls would blow up if they were baked."

As a birthday present, Janice presented John with a new pitching wedge. "He loved the present," said Janice. "But he wanted everyone to forget about his birthday, his age, and the golf balls." But the rest of the world wouldn't let him.

"Our local paper ran a story about the incident and the wire service picked it up," said Janice. "Soon I got calls from all over the country to do radio interviews. Even Paul Harvey mentioned it on his program. Everyone knew that my husband had turned thirty.

"All I had wanted to do was pull a little joke on John. Instead the joke was on me."

Practice Makes Imperfect

Strip Tees

Sam Snead once offered a few tips to a woman golfer, and she gave him the most memorable pointer of his life.

While she was taking practice swings, following Slammin' Sam's advice, Snead noticed a pink object working up from under her blouse toward her collar.

Suddenly, after an especially vigorous swing, one of her falsies flipped out and bounced on the ground. It did a few spins and settled on the grass pointing upward. Both stood speechless for a moment until Snead broke the silence by telling her, "That's okay. Just leave it there and use it for a tee." The woman was so mortified that she burst into tears and dashed off. Snead never saw her again.

Back to Reality

Peter Kostis, one of the most famous golf instructors in the world, has worked with the game's top pros. But his most memorable student was a woman who asked him for a lesson at Boca West Golf Course in Florida in 1983.

"She hit a seven-iron fat and popped it up," Kostis recalled. "Before the ball reached the ground, she hit it again on her follow-through. The ball went over her shoulder onto the tennis courts and rolled into the clubhouse that was under construction." It was a minus-70-yard shot.

"She teed up another one, undercut it again, and hit another pop-up that landed three yards in front of the tee and spun back to within a yard of her.

" 'That wasn't very good, was it?' she asked.

" 'Oh, I don't know,' I said. 'That was 69 yards longer than the last shot.'

"After working with the world's best players, I realized this was God's way of bringing me back to reality."

Curses to Those Courses

Sometimes a typographical error can be more accurate than the correct word.

A few years ago the state of North Carolina published a tourism booklet that promoted golf. In it there was this sentence: "Famous midsouth resorts include Pinehurst and Southern Pines, where it is said that there are more golf curses per square mile than anywhere else in the world."

Then again, maybe this wasn't a typo after all.

The Blind Leading the Blind

It's one thing to mark the ball on the green; it's quite another to mark a fishing spot.

In the summer of 1970, a few days before the U.S. Open at Chaska, Minnesota, two of golf's greatest gadflies, Chi Chi Rodriguez and Lee Trevino, rented a boat and went fishing together on a serene lake. They came upon a veritable spawning ground and pulled in one big bass after another.

As the sun began to set, Lee told Chi Chi to mark the spot in the lake so they could return the next day to continue their good fishing fortune. When they had docked, Lee asked Chi Chi if he had marked the spot. "Sure," Chi Chi replied. "I put a mark right here on the side of the boat."

Thunderstruck by this lack of common sense, Lee said, "That's a helluva thing to do. We may not get the same boat tomorrow."

WHO ELSE BELONGS IN THE GOLF HALL OF SHAME?

Do you have any nominations for *The Golf Hall of SHAME?* Give us your picks for the most shameful, zany, embarrassing, hilarious, and boneheaded moments in links history. Here's your opportunity to pay a lighthearted tribute to pros and duffers alike.

Those nominations that are documented with the greatest number of facts—such as firsthand accounts or newspaper or magazine clippings— have the best chance of being inducted into *The Golf Hall of SHAME.* Feel free to send as many nominations as you wish. (All submitted material becomes the property of *The Golf Hall of SHAME* and is nonreturnable.) If you have a nomination for any other sport, feel free to send that to us, too. Mail your nominations to:

> *The Golf Hall of SHAME*
> P.O. Box 31867
> Palm Beach Gardens, Florida 33420

THE DUFFERS

Bruce Nash gets lots of gimmes from his playing partners—"Gimme a break and get off the course!" He spends so much time in the sand traps that he packs a beach bucket and shovel in his golf bag. The only way that Bruce can drive a green is in a golf cart. His most infamous moment on the links came in 1978 at the Palm Beach (Florida) Golf Course when his heeled tee shot ricocheted off a nearby tree, bounced back, and nailed him in the butt.

Allan Zullo's most mortifying moment on the links happened in 1974 at the Barwick Golf Course in Delray Beach, Florida. He hooked his tee shot on the par-3 first hole and watched in horror as the ball headed for the third green where a fat lady in a dress was about to putt. Zullo's ball landed behind her and bounced up her dress—and didn't come out. Said Zullo's playing partner, Clyde Lang, loud enough for other golfers to hear, "Congratulations, Allan. Looks like you just got yourself a hole in one."